The price of war

TITLES OF RELATED INTEREST

★Not available from Allen & Unwin in North America

The price of war

URBANIZATION IN VIETNAM 1954–85

Nigel Thrift
*Saint David's University College,
University of Wales*

and

Dean Forbes
Australian National University

ALLEN AND UNWIN
Boston   Sydney

Allen & Unwin (Publishers) Ltd,
40 Museum Street, London WC1A 1LU, UK

Allen & Unwin (Publishers) Ltd,
Park Lane, Hemel Hempstead, Herts HP2 4TE, UK

Allen & Unwin, Inc.,
8 Winchester Place, Winchester, Mass. 01890, USA

Allen & Unwin (Australia) Ltd,
8 Napier Street, North Sydney, NSW 2060, Australia

First published in 1986

British Library Cataloguing in Publication Data

Thrift, Nigel
    The price of war : urbanization in Vietnam
    1954–85.
1. Urbanization——Vietnam——History——
20th century
I. Title   II. Forbes, Dean
307.7'6'09597   HT147.V5
ISBN 0 04 301210 8

Library of Congress Cataloging in Publication Data

Thrift, N. J.
    The price of war.
Bibliography: p.
Includes index.
1. Cities and towns——Vietnam——History——20th century.
2. Urbanization——Vietnam——History——20th century.
3. Vietnamese Conflict, 1961–1975.   I. Forbes, D. K.
(Dean K.)   II. Title
HT147.V5T48   1986   307.7'6'09597   86–3535
ISBN 0 04 301210 8 (alk. paper)

Set in 10 on 12 point Bembo by Phoenix Photosetting, Chatham
and printed in Great Britain by Billing and Sons Ltd,
London and Worcester.

For Lynda and Janet

A victory is the greatest tragedy in the world – except a defeat.

The Duke of Wellington

Preface and Acknowledgements

In October 1954 Ho Chi Minh returned to Hanoi, after eight years in the jungle, to set up a socialist state in the north of Vietnam. In April 1985 a 200 000-strong parade through the centre of Saigon, renamed Ho Chi Minh City in "Uncle" Ho's honour, marked the tenth anniversary of the fall of the premier city of the south of Vietnam to North Vietnamese forces. This monograph is an account of what happened to the towns and cities of Vietnam in the years between these two dates.

Considerable debts are always incurred in writing this kind of monograph. In particular, we should mention the help provided by that growing community of people interested in modern Vietnam. Nayan Chanda, Adam Fforde, Gerald Haberkorn, Gavin Jones, David Marr, Nguyen Duc Nhuan and Dan Vining all provided us with data and, in some cases, comments on the first draft of the manuscript. Anthony O'Connor provided us with detailed notes on the second draft. They are all, of course, absolved of any responsibility for the outcome. The Australian National University provided the funds for fieldwork in Vietnam. Keith Mitchell, Suzie Jeffcoat, Trevor Harris and Nigel Duffey drew the figures. Carol McKenzie and Maureen Hunwicks typed and retyped the manuscript. Barbara Banks provided research assistance.

We would like to thank the following organizations and individuals for permission to reproduce illustrative material:

G. W. Jones and the Centre for Development Studies, Australian National University (4.2, 8.1 & 2); Figure 4.3 reproduced from Nguyen Duc Nhuan 1984, Contraintes démographiques et politiques de développement au Vietnam 1975–1980, *Population* **36**, by permission of the author and Institut National d'Études Démographiques; Figure 4.4 reproduced from Elliott, D. 1981, Socialist Republic of Vietnam, in *Marxist governments: a world survey*, Vol. 3, B. Szajkowski (ed.), by permission of Macmillan, London and Basingstoke; J. R. Rogge and the Canadian Association of Geographers (8.3 & 4).

Finally, we wish to acknowledge the permission of Pion Ltd, publishers of *Environment and planning D. Society and space*, for allowing us to reproduce extracts from the paper "Cities, socialism and war" in the text.

Nigel Thrift
Dean Forbes

Contents

List of tables

1 Introduction

In the past 15 years "socialist" or "communist" states have come into existence at an increasing rate in the countries of the Third World (Fig. 1.1). The year 1983 was the high water mark. Seven of Africa's 50 independent black or Arab countries – Angola, Benin, the Congo, Ethiopia, Mozambique, Madagascar and Somalia – were self-professed Marxist–Leninist states. At least another eight – Algeria, the Cape Verde Islands, Libya, Guinea, Guinea-Bissau, Sao Tome and Principe, the Seychelles and Tanzania – embraced some form of socialism (Ottaway & Ottaway 1981). In Asia, the three Indochinese states of Kampuchea, Laos and Vietnam were controlled by Marxist–Leninist régimes, Burma continued to practise the Burmese way to socialism, and the inhabitants of North Korea lived under the "genetic socialism" of Kim Il Sung. Outside Africa and Asia socialist states were less common; however, in Central America Nicaragua had become a test of the strength of the United

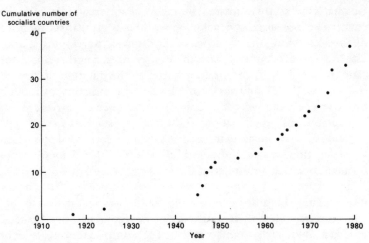

Figure 1.1 The increasing number of socialist countries.

States, and in the Caribbean there were Cuba and Grenada. South America seemed to form a bulwark against bolshevism but, even here, the example of Guyana prevented any overhasty generalizations.

It is only natural that, in these circumstances, this new socialist Third World has become the subject of an ever-increasing number of studies in subjects like economics, politics and strategic studies (e.g. Donaldson 1981, Feuchtwangler & Nailor 1981, Ottaway & Ottaway 1981, Szajkowski 1981, Chase-Dunn 1982, Wiles 1982) as well as, of course, in development studies (e.g. White & White 1982, Wilber & Jameson 1982, White et al. 1983).

This book is concerned with the subject of urbanization in the countries of this new socialist Third World, or as we prefer to call them, the "actually existing socialist"[1] developing countries (hereafter referred to as the "socialist developing countries"). Clearly such a subject is large and complex. The result is that in this monograph only the most tentative of conclusions can be drawn. There are all sorts of reasons for our state of caution, but four stand out and these problem areas form the main content of the first two chapters of this monograph.

To begin with, the socialist developing countries are not all alike. If the differences between Yugoslavia and Angola or Romania and Guyana are great enough to justify the existence of a separate category of socialist developing countries, this does not mean that Angola and Guyana are exactly similar. The range of differences among the countries of the socialist developing world is as great as the range of differences among the countries of the capitalist developing world. The first part of Chapter 2 charts these differences. Another reason for caution is that the theoretical backdrop to the question of how to characterize these countries is complex and contradictory. Although the overwhelming weight of opinion is that such countries are not (except by self-proclamation) full-blooded "socialist" states, the question of what precisely these countries are is not helped by such an act of negation. Indeed, if anything, a whole new host of questions are opened up which a number of the existing, monolithic theories of socialism are wont to suppress. A framework is needed that can take into account the differences among the non-capitalist developing countries, as well as their similarities. The second part of Chapter 2 tries to provide such a framework, concentrating on the categories of state, economy, civil society and external relations.

A third reason for our state of caution concerns the condition of the urban and regional data on non-capitalist developing countries. These data are often uncollected or may be unavailable. However, when they are available, they are likely to be incomplete, unreliable or out of date (although, in this respect, the situation is not so very different from that found in a number of capitalist developing countries). This means that a consideration of the differences in patterns and processes of urbanization among these countries is a task fraught with danger, although no less necessary for that. The first part of Chapter 3 represents just such a consideration. Finally, too many of the supposedly theoretical concepts that have been put forward to explain these patterns and processes of urbanization – concepts like "de-urbanization" or "underurbanization" – have been simply broad comparative descriptions of what is happening in the urban realm of these countries relative to what is happening in the urban realm of other countries. Not that this is so surprising. A critic might suggest that the present situation is rather like trying to write down an equation where some of the terms are almost certainly missing and others remain undefined or are defined in such a way that their meaning is obscured. The second part of Chapter 3 presents, in the context provided by the previous discussion, an attempt to answer this criticism via the general model of urbanization under socialism outlined by Murray and Szelenyi (1984). This model is intended to apply to the process of urbanization in *all* socialist countries. As will be shown, the model therefore gives insufficient attention to the specific circumstances of the socialist *developing* countries with the result that some important determinants of urbanization in these countries are omitted.

In the second part of the monograph some of the limited insights gained in the first part are put to work in considering the specific case of the history of the larger towns and cities[2] of Vietnam under socialism from 1954 through to 1985. Apart from its intrinsic interest, Vietnam also forms a useful benchmark in the study of socialist developing countries. Thus the North has had a "socialist" existence long enough to reveal some of the longer-term tendencies and difficulties faced by such societies, and the incorporation of the South after reunification in 1975 provides a useful means by which to study the course and impacts of socialist policies in a period when many socialist developing countries came into being.

Chapter 4 contains a general introduction to some of the basic aspects of Vietnam; especially its history, economy, demography and administrative structure. Chapter 5 is an analysis of the form of the state, economy, civil society and external relations of the Democratic Republic of Vietnam from its founding in the north of the country in 1954 to the reunification with the South in 1975. Chapter 6 considers the history and pattern of urbanization in the Democratic Republic in this period through the categories of the aforementioned Murray–Szelenyi model. Chapters 7 and 8 repeat this exercise for the Socialist Republic of Vietnam from its founding in 1976 to 1985, with emphasis on what happened in the south of the country during this period. Chapter 9 is an attempt to place some flesh on the bare bones of the accounts of the preceding four chapters through a consideration of the history under socialism of two particular large Vietnamese cities: Hanoi in the north of the country and Ho Chi Minh City[3] in the south.[4] Finally Chapter 10 presents some brief conclusions concerning the utility of the set of theoretical categories that have been deployed in this monograph in the light of the Vietnamese experience of urbanization under socialism. In particular, the importance of warfare, or the threat of it, in determining the course of Vietnamese urbanization is stressed. The cities of Vietnam have paid the price of war.[5]

A NOTE ON DATA

Data on Vietnam are hard to come by. Records relating to particular places or times are often incomplete. Sometimes in order to build up as complete a picture as possible, it has been necessary to amalgamate data from different sources which, for reasons of changing methods of collection, or different ways of calculating estimates, may be only partly compatible. Data may also contain errors about which we have not been informed.

Indication is given where data are derived from censuses or official surveys, and also where data are only estimates. Where data from different sources disagree (and this is surprisingly rare), we have taken the lower value.

Needless to say these caveats mean that the data we offer on Vietnam and Vietnamese urbanization must be treated with caution. However, the fact is that the data we use are often all the data there are.

One further caveat: a period of protracted fieldwork in particular towns and cities would be necessary to deal with certain issues concerning Vietnamese urbanization – for example, the internal structure of the cities or patterns of everyday life. However, such fieldwork is extremely difficult to arrange and our field experience of Vietnam has been on a more modest scale. Therefore, as a general principle we have adopted the rule: whereof we do not know, we do not speak.

Notes

1 The term "socialist" is employed only because it is in common usage to identify the kind of countries that are the subject of this monograph. We toyed with the idea of employing terms like "non-capitalist" or "actually existing socialist" throughout the monograph but they seemed too clumsy. On the whole we concur with Castoriadis' (1973, p. 67) judgement that:

> it is not capitalism, it is not socialism, it is not even on its way to these two forms; the socialist economy represents a historically new type, and its name matters little if its essential features are understood.

2 Our focus on the larger towns and cities of Vietnam is entirely pragmatic: information on small towns and villages is very hard to come by, with the exception of a few specific studies of particular villages (e.g. Trullinger 1980, Houtart & Lemercinier 1984).

3 Throughout the monograph, we have followed the convention of referring to this city as Saigon in pre-reunification Vietnam and Ho Chi Minh City post-reunification.

4 A monograph of this type is not the place to bring in all the impressionistic fieldwork experience that it is possible to draw upon. However, it is worth noting the comparisons in this vein of Hanoi and Ho Chi Minh City by Shawcross (1981), McCoy (1983), Forbes and Thrift (1984) and Shaplen (1985a, b).

5 We have taken a decision to omit diacritical marks on the Vietnamese names in this monograph for reasons of typographical convenience. Apologies to those who may be offended.

2 The problems of characterizing socialist developing countries[1]

What is it that is distinctive about socialist developing countries? This chapter tries to answer this difficult question in two parts. The first part of the chapter serves as an empirical prolegomenon, via what comparative data are available, to the second part of the chapter in which we try to come to terms with the extant theoretical literature on socialist[2] societies in the context of developing countries.

Empirical characteristics

An obvious place to start an investigation of socialist developing countries is by distinguishing between capitalist and socialist countries. However, such is the difficulty of the investigation that problems emerge even at this very preliminary stage.

Figure 2.1 and Table 2.1 show the countries that might be considered as socialist, according to the following criteria:

(a) effective one-party rule;

(b) socialism and socialist goals written into the constitution;

(c) a high and increasing degree of state ownership of industry;

(d) a high and increasing degree of state ownership of agriculture (through state farms) and/or the collectivization of agriculture;

(e) evidence of at least the beginnings of a centralized "command" economy.

Clearly these criteria do not surmount the problems of characterizing opportunist régimes like Kerekou's Benin or the late Forbes Burnham's Guyana (Decalo 1981, Racine 1982), or countries like the all but one-party African states of Zambia and Zimbabwe that are (and an agricultural sector generally able to keep pace with this growth), relatively high GNP *per capita* and a large industrial sector. In contrast, most of the socialist "developing" countries have all the classical indicators associated with their capitalist counterparts: high rates of population growth (and an agricultural sector generally unable to keep pace with increases in demand), generally low GNP *per capita* and a large agricultural sector.

However, a second more complex grouping is perhaps more adequate (Fig. 2.2, Table 2.3). Following Wiles and Smith (1981) and Wiles (1982), it is possible to differentiate among four groups of socialist countries.

Group 1:   Countries that are full members of the Council of Mutual Economic Assistance (CMEA or COMECON), subdivided into (a) the "European" core consisting of the USSR and its satellites, and (b) "non-European" members.

Group 2:   Countries that have been "communist" or "socialist" for some time, but which are not under the influence of the USSR.

Group 3:   Countries that have proclaimed hard-line socialist forms of government and generally have close relationships with the USSR or are occupied by military forces belonging to the USSR or its satellites. These countries are under one-party rule and are relatively stable (with the exception of Afghanistan).

Group 4:   The "marginals" are countries that have usually only recently declared themselves to be socialist and which, like Chile, Jamaica or Grenada, may well revert to a capitalist system. They are examples of Kalecki's (1972) "intermediate" economies (see Jameson 1980). These countries can be further subdivided into (a) those countries which are avowedly Marxist–Leninist and are therefore quite close to the countries of Group 3 (although often lacking these countries' even marginal stability) and (b) those countries which are effectively in the hands of a one-party "socialist" state. Most of the countries in this group follow "non-doctrinaire" forms of socialism and some still have a substantial petty commodity producing or even capitalist sector.

However, this kind of classificatory exercise can take us only so far. In particular, it does not take into account the differential resource endowments of each of those countries. For example, in Africa the countries of Tanzania, Ethiopia and Guinea-Bissau are poor in such endowments by any standards, but Algeria, Libya, Angola and

Table 2.2 Basic indicators for socialist countries.

	Population 1981	Population growth (%) 1960–70	Population growth (%) 1970–80	Area (1000 km²)	GNP (US $ millions) 1980	Per capita average annual growth rate (%) 1960–80
Kampuchea	6.9	2.6	−0.2	181	—	—
Laos	3.4	1.9	1.8	237	—	—
Ethiopia	31.1	2.4	2.0	1222	140	1.4
Somalia	3.9	2.4	2.3	638	—	—
Guinea-Bissau	0.8	—	—	36	160	—
Burma	34.8	2.3	2.4	677	170	1.2
Afghanistan	15.9	2.2	2.5	648	—	—
Vietnam	54.2	3.1	2.8	330	—	—
Mozambique	12.1	2.1	4.0	802	230	−0.1
Tanzania	18.7	2.7	3.4	945	280	1.9
China	976.7	1.9	1.8	9561	290	—
Guinea	5.4	2.8	2.9	246	290	0.3
Cape Verde	0.3	—	—	4	300	—
Benin	3.4	2.5	2.6	113	310	0.4
Madagascar	8.7	2.1	2.5	587	350	−0.5
Yemen, People's Democratic Republic of	1.9	2.1	2.4	333	420	12.1
Angola	7.1	1.5	2.4	1247	470	−2.3
Sao Tome & Principe	0.1	—	—	1	490	0.3
mean*	14.8	2.3	2.4	586	296	1.6
Grenada	0.8	—	—	<1	690	1.6
Guyana	0.1	—	—	215	690	0.9
Nicaragua	2.6	2.6	3.4	130	790	0.9
Congo	1.6	1.6	2.4	342	900	0.8
Mongolia	1.7	1.7	2.9	1565	1290	—
Albania	2.7	2.7	2.8	29	—	—
Korea, Democratic Republic of	18.3	2.9	2.6	121	—	—
Syria	9.0	3.2	3.6	185	1340	3.7
Cuba	9.7	2.0	1.3	115	—	—
Seychelles	0.1	—	—	1	1770	3.1
Algeria	18.9	2.4	3.2	2382	1870	3.2
Iraq	13.1	3.1	3.3	435	3020	5.3
mean†	8.6	2.5	2.8	589	1526	2.8
Romania	22.2	1.0	0.9	238	2340	8.6
Yugoslavia	22.3	1.0	0.9	256	2620	5.4
Poland	35.8	1.0	0.9	313	3900	5.3
Bulgaria	9.0	0.8	0.6	111	4150	5.6
Hungary	10.8	0.4	0.4	93	4180	4.5
USSR	265.5	1.2	0.9	22402	4550	4.0
Czechoslovakia	15.3	0.5	0.7	128	5820	4.0
Germany, Democratic Republic of	16.9	−0.1	−0.1	108	7180	4.7
Libya	3.0	3.8	4.1	1760	8640	5.2
mean‡	18.9	0.7	0.6	178	4313	5.4

* Excludes China, Guinea-Bissau, Cape Verde, Sao Tome and Principe.
† Excludes Grenada, Guyana and Seychelles.
‡ Excludes USSR and Libya.
Sources: Central Intelligence Agency (1981), *Far Eastern Economic Review* Yearbook (1981), World Bank (1982).

GDP		GDP (%) 1980				Per cent labour force in industry 1980	Average index of food production per capita 1978–80 (1969–71 = 100)
1960	1980	agriculture	industry	(manufacturing)	services		
—	—	—	—	—	—	—	41
—	—	—	—	—	—	6	100
900	3690	60	11	7	29	7	83
160	1130	46	13	10	41	8	84
—	—	—	—	—	—	—	91
1280	5550	—	—	—	—	10	99
1190	—	—	—	—	—	8	95
—	—	—	—	—	—	10	107
830	2360	44	16	9	40	18	75
550	4350	54	13	9	33	6	92
—	252 230	31	47	—	22	17	116
370	1670	37	33	4	30	11	86
—	—	—	—	—	—	—	—
160	950	43	12	7	45	16	99
540	3260	36	18	—	46	3	95
—	540	13	28	14	59	15	103
690	2500	48	23	3	29	19	82
—	—	—	—	—	—	—	—
667	2600	42	18	8	39	10	89
—	—	—	—	—	—	—	—
—	—	—	—	—	—	—	—
340	2120	23	31	25	46	14	95
130	1750	12	45	6	43	26	79
—	—	—	—	—	—	22	97
—	—	—	—	—	—	25	104
—	—	—	—	—	—	33	133
890	12 900	20	27	21	53	31	157
—	—	—	—	—	—	31	105
—	—	—	—	—	—	—	—
2740	39 870	6	57	14	37	25	80
1580	35 810	7	73	6	19	26	90
1136	18 490	14	47	14	40	26	104
—	57 650	11	64	—	25	36	145
9860	62 100	12	43	30	45	35	115
—	—	15	64	—	21	39	102
—	—	17	58	—	25	39	114
—	—	14	59	—	27	53	130
—	—	16	62	—	22	45	108
—	—	8	75	—	19	48	115
—	—	9	70	—	21	50	126
310	32 090	2	72	4	26	28	139
—	—	12	62	—	26	43	121

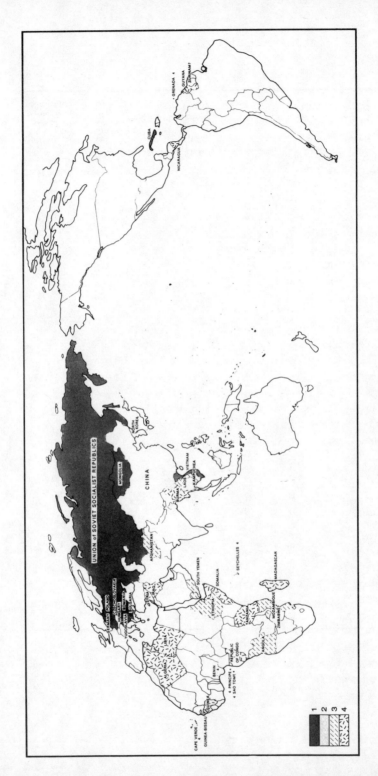

Figure 2.2 The socialist countries of the world in 1983: the Wiles classification.

Guinea have natural resources which make them presently or potentially amongst that continent's richest nations. Neither does the classification do more than nod in the direction of the strategic importance of these societies to the USSR and the USA, an importance that continually changes.[5] However, it is possible to doubt that any classification can finally take into account the diversity of these countries unless it is backed up by some theoretical consideration of the nature of the societies involved. This we now attempt.

Theoretical characterization

A theoretical approach to the problem of characterizing socialist developing countries must consider, above all else, the Marxist characterization of socialist economy and society. There is a very simple reason for this focus. The only coherent theoretical expositions of this kind of economy and society have all been influenced by the works of Marx and Lenin in one way or another.

There are other reasons, as well, for the primacy of Marxist theory in the analysis of socialist societies. First, most of these societies are founded on or at least pay lip-service to Marxist-Leninist principles. Secondly, many of the extant theoretical debates have sprung out of the *practical* problems involved in trying to implement these principles. Thirdly, any flaws in current interpretations of Marxist theory are likely to be amplified in practice, requiring some degree of reformulation in the theory.

PROBLEMS IN MARXIST INTERPRETATIONS

There are obvious difficulties in attempting any reconstruction of what Marx regarded as socialism (the "dictatorship of the proletariat")[6] and "full" communism, since Marx's writings on these subjects do not form any coherent whole. His thoughts are scattered through various works, vary with time and are sometimes contradictory. There are at least two reasons for this state of affairs. First, Marx had an almost pathological fear of utopianism. Secondly, he never found the time to attempt a complete formulation of his theory. Whatever the reason the result is the same. As Engels put it in a letter to Marx (cited in Ollman 1977, p. 8), "the famous 'positive', what you 'really' want" was never written. Numerous books and

Table 2.3 The socialist countries of the the world in 1983: the Wiles classification. Figures in brackets are dates of first "socialist" government coming to power, through peaceful transition or coup rather than formal declaration.

Group 1: full members of the CMEA

(a) European

USSR (1917)
Bulgaria, P.R. (1947)
Czechoslovakia S.R. (1948)
Germany, D.R. (1945)
Hungary, P.R. (1946)
Poland, P.R. (1947)
Romania, S.R. (1947)

(b) Non-European

Cuba, R. (1959)
Mongolia, P.R. (1924)
Vietnam, S.R. (1954)

Group 2: non-CMEA but socialist for a long time

Albania, S.P.R. (1946)
China, P.R. (1949)
Korea, D.R. (1945)
Yugoslavia, S.F.R. (1945)

Group 3: socialist developing countries (all avowed Marxist–Leninist)

Afghanistan (1978)
Angola, P.R. (1975)
Kampuchea, D. (1975)
Ethiopia (1974)
Laos, P.D.R. (1975)
Mozambique, P.R. (1975)
Yemen, P.D.R. (1967)

Group 4: "marginals"

(a) Avowed Marxist–Leninist

Benin, P.R. (1972)
Congo, P.R. (1979)
Somalia, D.R. (1969)

(b) One-party "socialist"

Algeria, P.R. (1965)
Burma, S.R. (1974)
Cape Verde, R. (1974)
Grenada, R. (1979–1984)
Guinea, R. (1958)
Guinea-Bissau, R. (1974)
Guyana (1970)
Iraq, A.S.R. (1963)
Libya, S.P. (1969)
Madagascar, D.R. (1975)
Nicaragua, P.R. (1979)
Sao Tome and Principe, D.R. (1975)
Seychelles, R. (1979)
Syria, A.S.R. (1963)
Tanzania, U.R. (1964)

A.S.R., Arab Socialist Republic; D., Democratic; D.R., Democratic Republic; P.R., People's Republic; P.D.R., People's Democratic Republic; S.F.R., Socialist Free Republic; S.P.R., Socialist People's Republic; S.R., Socialist Republic; R., Republic; S.P., Socialist People; U.R., United Republic.

Sources: Paxton (1981), Szajkowski (1981), Wiles (1982).

papers have been devoted to reconstructing this "famous positive" and although there are many disagreements over what measures Marx thought were necessary to mount a socialist programme and what the results might be, there is enough common ground in recent works on the subject (e.g. Ollman 1977, Bahro 1978, Selucky 1979, Bienkowski 1981, Frankel 1983, Nove 1983) to permit the following points to be made.

Marx saw socialism as arising out of the socialized production characteristic of the then new forms of capitalism: the joint-stock company and the monopolies, the social organization of labour and the establishment of a world market. In much of his writing the abolition of private property can be seen as almost a part of a natural process of the maturation of capitalism, with socialism inevitably following the expropriation of the capitalists. This socialism would be built upon the extant infrastructure of socialized production although now without the impediments of capitalism; thus wealth based on the value form would disappear, wage labour would wither, money would cease to exist, and so on. Of course, what Marx foresaw has not come into existence, except in caricature. He greatly underestimated the tenacity of capitalism in countries with a strong capitalist economy, and it was not until late in his life, with his interest in Russia, that he realized that a socialist programme might be adopted in countries with less developed capitalist economies and small industrial proletariats. In both cases, however, Marx critically underestimated what we will call the problem of *implementation*, that is the actual mechanics of how a socialist order will be put into place after a capitalist or non–capitalist ruling order has been displaced in the face of *continuing scarcities and shortages* (for example, in the production and distribution of food), *continuing inequalities* (like patriarchy, the division between mental and manual workers, and an unequal spatial distribution of population) and *continuing pre-revolutionary social relations* (like tribes and religions) (see, for example, Bahro 1978, Szelenyi 1978, Konrad & Szelenyi 1979, Vajda 1981).

It is obviously neither possible nor necessary to provide, in the space of this monograph, a review of every attempt to recast Marx's vision of socialism from Kautsky and Lenin onwards (especially as the problems of implementation became clearer) or the more recent attempts by Marxist writers to explain the societies that Lenin and others founded. Instead we have tried to combine this literature into a very general account of socialist societies. This account attempts to incorporate the sometimes crucial influence of scarcities, inequalities and pre-revolutionary social relations on the history of these societies. It also tries to avoid some of the pitfalls found in extant Marxist writings on socialist societies, namely *evolutionism, reductionism* and the *too easy identification of socialist ideology with the characteristics of these societies*. These pitfalls are expanded upon briefly below.

Armed with the assumption that societies "evolve", all "actually existing socialist" societies (note the supposition here) can be seen as either in the transition to "ideal" socialism or, alternatively, as sliding back into capitalism and therefore "deformed". The goal of history, in other words, is already established. The only problem is to find out when the ball is going to hit the net of socialism, why it hasn't already done so, or why it is running back the other way. The three major Marxist approaches to the explanation of the USSR and allied societies (see Nuti 1979) all share this problem of evolutionism (although they are significantly different in other respects). Thus, the orthodox Trotskyist line (e.g. Mandel 1974) regards actually existing socialist societies as transitional between capitalism and socialism, and the USSR, for example, as a "bureaucratically deformed workers' state". In contrast, the international socialist line (e.g. Cliff 1964) regards the Soviet Union (and other societies such as Maoist China and North Korea) as "bureaucratic state-capitalist". The Maoist line (e.g. Bettelheim 1975) is that the Soviet Union and societies like it are "state-capitalist".

The reductionism that is apparent in a number of Marxist approaches to socialist countries stems from a number of assumptions, but most particularly from the depiction of societies as ordered totalities in which determination can act as a set of direct, unmediated, even remorseless connections. This tendency is most apparent, of course, in Marxist work on the state under capitalism, where the state is all too often reduced to an instrument of the dominant economic class, automatically changing its form in response to the needs of the capitalist system (see Urry 1981). A similar tendency can be found in work on *civil society* (that set of practices which lie outside the state and economy, through which individuals are socialized and by which an individual's individuality is formed according to such diverse influences as gender, age, geography and race):[7] for example, the family, gender relations, and so on can all be derived from the dictates of capital (see Cohen 1982).

This same tendency to reductionism (and functionalism) can be found in writings on socialist societies, but here the superordinate status of capital is transferred to the state. However, to say that the state is determinant in socialist societies does not mean that all human life is sucked into its orbit and there regimented solely for the benefit of a state bureaucracy. In particular, it is important not to confuse the extent of the state's activities in these societies with effectiveness: for example, it has been disputed whether "planned" economies are truly planned at all (see Zaleski 1980). The often fragmented and chaotic circumstances of many socialist developing countries only underline the force of this admonition.

Finally, Marxist attempts to characterize non-capitalist societies have often been subject to a premature association of socialist (and, in particular, Leninist) ideology and the analysis of socialist societies. Although the influence of such ideology has clearly been great within these societies, it does not automatically follow that all post-revolutionary changes stem from the implementation of that ideology (see Nove 1983): for example, current Eastern European regional management systems seem to trace their roots from pre-revolutionary Eastern European history rather than from explicit socialist programmes (see Szelenyi 1981b, Rev 1984). Nevertheless, they can, of course, be *justified* by reference to Marx or Lenin.

How, then, to obtain a view of socialist societies that is neither evolutionist, reductionist or fundamentalist? This task is the subject of the next section which is an attempt to draw upon recent Marxist and neo-Marxist writings without, however, becoming a slave to them.

AN ALTERNATIVE INTERPRETATION

Most modern societies can be thought to consist of three interacting "spheres" – "civil society", the state and the economy (Urry 1981) – each with its own distinctive forms of exploitation (Fig. 2.3).[8] Each of these three spheres can become determinant in different places at different times. *Civil society*, the realm of practices, has always existed as a number of rudimentary forms of social organization – the tribe, the region, religion, race, the family, and so on – around a number of which nationalist tendencies (which have been so important in many "socialist" revolutions) can crystallize. Already built into civil society are certain forms of exploitation, for

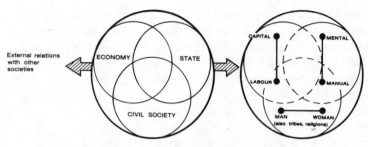

Figure 2.3 The three spheres of society.

instance that of gender. Historically, the *state* has tended to become the next sphere that is determinant. The power of the state is primarily based upon the division between mental and manual labour, but also relies on other divisions like that between town and country, and, of course, the invention of techniques that enable these divisions to be maintained, always backed up by physical coercion (see Giddens 1981). For example, in the 18th and 19th centuries the state, through all manner of new institutions like the civil service, the census and the police, was able to become an ever more potent force as it extended a "grid of intelligibility" over society and penetrated everyday life (although this tendency was rooted in much earlier situations) (see Foucault 1972, 1977, Elias 1982, Thrift 1983). Then, in the late 18th and early 19th centuries it became possible for the *economy* to be determinant as self-expanding capital emerged as a force to be reckoned with. Power came from the employment of "free" abstract or capital-producing labour. Finally, each modern society has *external* relations with other types of society: that is, each society exists in conjunction with, and sometimes interdependently, with other types of society and these interactions can have important effects on the form state, economy and civil society can take (Skocpol 1979).[9] Currently, the competition between capitalist and noncapitalist societies, in both economic and military terms (in so far as these can be separated), is the most influential of these relations, especially the consequent connection of societies with the USSR or the USA (White 1984).

The common feature of socialist societies is the formation (or the attempt at the formation) of a determinant, strong state (Fig. 2.4). This strong state is run by a state "class"[10] made up of the upper echelons of the government, party and army from which the

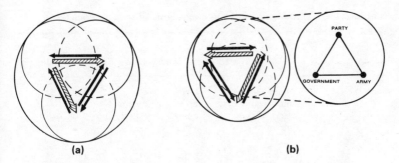

Figure 2.4 Determination in (a) capitalist and (b) socialist societies.

majority of the society is excluded by reason of lack of qualifications, lack of access to the necessary channels of social mobility, and so on (Fig. 2.5). At least three stages have been identified in the formation of such a state-determined society (G. White 1983) in each of which there are corresponding changes in the way the economy is run, in the importance of civil society, in the make-up of classes other than the state class[11] and in the composition of the state class itself. The chief characteristics of these three stages form a simple "ideal type" model (Table 2.4) although all the usual caveats pertaining to this form of model must be applied. In addition, these stages should not be thought of as parts of a necessary, evolutionary sequence or as occupying fixed periods of time: rather, the model is a simple synthetic device. We shall concentrate in the following account on the form that the state and state class take in each stage.

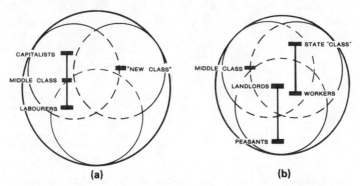

Figure 2.5 Class structure in (a) capitalist and (b) socialist societies.

Table 2.4 A simple model of the dimensions of socialist societies.

Sphere	"Revolutionary"	Stage "Bureaucratic"	"Technocratic"(?)
state	based on mass mobilization and old wartime methods	formation of government bureaucracy, party and army	—
economy	collectivization of agriculture; crash programme of industrialization attempted; nationalization of existing industry; abolition or limitation of markets; extreme scarcity	industrialized, centrally planned economy with periods of freeze and thaw in market relations; periods of scarcity, continual shortages	complex economy; need to satisfy consumer aspiration of population because of chronic shortages
civil society	still very important; tribal, religious divisions abound	less important as mass education systems and other state institutions are put into place	—
class composition within state "class"	revolutionaries and cadre leaders	revolutionaries vs bureaucracy; bureaucracy takes over from revolutionaries	bureaucracy vs new technocrats
other classes	capitalist and entrepreneurial middle class destroyed; small industrial working class; peasantry largest class numerically	larger industrial working class	industrial working class now very important; "service class" becoming more important
external relations with other societies	extreme threat from external forces; often have to take on status of client state to survive	becomes formal part of communist bloc	yearning to escape *some* of the constraints of the communist bloc

In the first, "revolutionary" stage, a state is needed in order to grapple with the immediate problems of post-revolutionary implementation and, in particular:

(a) the destruction of antagonistic class forces. Immediately, this will mean not only the removal of an indigenous capitalist class,[6] but also an attempt to rid society of any entrepreneurial middle class. The Leninist dictum that the petty bourgeoisie "generates capitalism every day, every hour, every minute" is taken very seriously (and continues to be taken seriously in all other stages);

(b) the production of scarce food in what are almost always, at this stage, predominantly agricultural societies;

(c) high levels of internal and external threat (the two often being linked). Often the new state will be at war both with separatist movements within its own borders and with neighbouring countries.

In these circumstances, mass mobilization is important and revolutionary methods, often based upon wartime organization, are still used not least because there are usually so few cadres per head of population and those that exist often lack the necessary administrative skills. (As Lenin put it, "ninety per cent of communists are not competent to carry out their functions".) Indeed, quite often, skilled administrative manpower is in such short supply that the previous state's administrative structure and personnel has to be incorporated. The embryonic state class is usually composed of the original core of leading revolutionaries and the enthusiastic young leaders of the revolutionary cadres.

Over time, however, the state begins to become more formal and starts to function as "the taskmaster of society in its technical and social modernization" (Bahro 1978, p. 129). In this second, "bureaucratic" stage the state's power is guaranteed by four factors in particular. First, in line with the prevailing ideology, many socialist societies have tried (or are still trying) to establish a productive, state-owned industrial base, rather than reap its legacy, often against a background of collectivization and state ownership of agriculture. In the absence of a capitalist sector and a market these imperatives require extensive *centralized planning* which leads to an equally extensive bureaucracy.

Centralized planning is, by itself, enough to guarantee the existence of a strong state since it necessarily generates a vast government bureaucracy that acts as a substitute for the market. For example, in the USSR (an admittedly extreme case):

> there are 12 million identifiably different products (disaggregated down to specific types of ball-bearings, designs of cloth, size of brown shoes, and so on). There are close to 50,000 industrial establishments plus, of course, thousands of construction enterprises, transport undertakings, collective and state farms, wholesaling organs and retail outlets. None of them can produce or distribute anything without the co-ordinated cooperation of the activities of numerous economic units which produce, transport or distribute (Nove 1983, p. 33).

Each of these elements has to be incorporated into a *plan*. Each plan has a set of *plan instructions* which have to be expressed in units of measurement (often a difficult enough task in itself) and to which *indicators* of success or failure in terms of output have to be attached. Some 2700–3600 of these indicators are determined at all levels of the Soviet system each year, 10% of which are determined by the central authorities. In any instance where there is a product mix, these indicators must be aggregated. In the average five-year plan there will be 48 000 of these aggregated *plan positions*. Furthermore, each of the aggregated products which is the subject of a plan instruction is, on average, an aggregation of 250 subproducts. The sheer scale of this system, in terms of the information required, the degree of organization needed to make it work and the subsidiary organization that is need to combat shortages and the other inefficiencies that are inevitably introduced (see Brus 1972, 1975; Ellman 1979; Kornai 1980; Nove 1983) is enough to guarantee the presence of a vast bureaucracy without invoking any idea of a plot by a state class to extend its power. Moreover, it is not surprising that the "bureaucratic" stage economy tends to go through periods of freeze and thaw of free market relations (see Nuti 1979). In part, this can be seen as simply a desire to unload some of the workload the bureaucracy must bear.[12]

Secondly, attempts are made to institute a new type of centralized *culture*, especially through an expanded educational system. Such a culture is increasingly needed as the new state and industrial economy take root and grow, in order to supply the state and economy with skilled individuals (see Gellner 1983).

Thirdly, most revolutionary movements are run by actual or *de facto* Leninist vanguards which, after the revolution, become incorporated into the state as the party. This party often becomes not much more than an executive arm of government, even duplicating some of its functions.

Finally, most revolutionary movements have mobilized a revolutionary army and, for reasons of internal security and external threat, must maintain and placate it long after its initial use and purpose may have faded. Thus, the armed forces become an inextricable part of the state (see Bienkowski 1981, MacKenzie 1983) and a permanent arms economy is ranged in opposition to capitalist (and other socialist) societies. The three main elements of the non-capitalist strong state, then, are the apparatuses of the government, the party and the army.

In the absence of a capitalist class, the state becomes the source of power and the primary interest of its members in its everyday reproduction inevitably reproduces that power (Castoriadis 1973, 1980; Lefort 1974). A process of gradual state expansion (what Fanon has called the process of "oligarchic bureaucratization") goes on, one in which the bureaucracy becomes ever more extensive. As time goes by the original revolutionaries are replaced by bureaucrats who have risen to power according to newly canalized and rapidly institutionalized channels of social mobility. The strategic rôle in the bureaucracy is played by an educated urban élite.

Finally, there is some evidence of a third "technocratic" stage in the development of some of the more advanced Eastern European societies (most notably Hungary), in which a new group of technocrats springing from an entirely post-revolutionary environment develops a critique of, interests in and designs on the state which bring it into conflict with the traditional bureaucratic élite. In particular, as the socialist economy becomes more complex and less skeletal, as the demands for consumer goods and a less spartan life-style grow, and as traditional methods of directive planning (based on production for investment for production) start to appear inadequate, so this new group's hand is strengthened. However, it is still too early to tell whether this élite can transform itself into an "intelligentsia on the road to class power"[13] as is sometimes supposed (e.g. Gouldner 1979, Konrad & Szelenyi 1979). Certainly no non-capitalist society seems to have as yet convincingly reached this stage.

Of course, no socialist society will fit easily and unproblematically into this three-stage model, either in terms of following the sequence exactly (or at all) or in terms of conforming exactly with the main features of each stage. Nevertheless, that there is some degree of fit can be shown by considering the two poles of the current pattern of socialist countries: the "European core" of socialist developed countries and the many recently founded and still struggling socialist developing countries.

With the obvious exception of the USSR, most of the socialist developed countries were founded in the aftermath of World War II upon an extant productive base. They have now been in existence for many years and possess a formal *state* apparatus which is in place and reproducing itself. They are classical examples of the "bureaucratic" stage in that they have an extensive government bureaucracy and a developed party machine, both of which have reached the second generation and have therefore started to become naturalized in the eyes of the population as a whole. These societies have an extensive internal security apparatus and they have reached an accommodation with the army. With the exception of Yugoslavia, the *economy* is centrally planned: that is "the ultimate decisions on priorities, on capital investment, as targets for sectoral and spatial patterns of growth and change, and on means of achieving these targets, are taken by state organizations, primarily by the central organs of government and party" (French & Hamilton 1979, p. 4). Further, targets are set which have at least some chance of being reached. *Civil society* has been extensively penetrated. Trade unions, for example, are simply arms of the state. Education is firmly controlled. This penetration is never completed, of course: witness the power of the Catholic church in Poland, for example. However, such organizations have usually reached an accommodation with the state, however uneasy it may sometimes be. Finally, *external relations* are controlled by membership of the Soviet bloc. The reliance of most of these socialist developed countries on the USSR and each other must be deemed a point of strength (as well as a source of weakness).

In contrast, in many of the recently founded socialist developing countries the establishment of the state as determinant is often still problematic. They are still very much in the "revolutionary" stage. The *state* bureaucracy is usually only part-formed and often lacks even basic skills. The relation between the government bureaucracy, the party and the army is often uneasy. The army may be in control.

Added to this, the *economy* may still have capitalist elements (especially those of international capital) or, in the process of being collectivized, may be being mismanaged, especially in terms of productivity. *Civil society* still exerts an extremely powerful influence. Whether the influence takes the form of tribal strife, regional separatist tendencies or religious divides, the state may well not be in control of these elements or it may itself be saturated by them to the extent that the allegiance of the bureaucracy to a socialist state can be questioned.[14]

Finally, *external relations* are extremely problematic. Some 200 "small" wars have been fought since the end of World War II (Shaw 1984), mostly between Third World countries, at the cost of 25 million dead. Moreover, this figure excludes other forms of military activity such as incursions from hostile states, subversion and other lesser threats. Military conflict creates a particular set of national priorities, an inevitable drain upon scarce resources and a high "military participation ratio" (Andreski 1968, Marwick 1968) – the proportion of the population of a society mobilized for war – which when put together can have considerable implications for *internal* development strategies. At one level, sustained military conflict can be seen as simply the result of internecine struggles between nation–states (Douglas 1985); however, at another level, it must be seen as part of the continuing tension between the two superpowers.[15] Indeed, such are the political, economic and ideological pressures on many socialist Third World countries as a result of this tension that:

> all their internal processes will, in one way or another be "forced" by the changing balance of international forces and relations. From the point of view of development theory, this creates a fundamental obstacle to the formulation of generalisations on the basis of their internal social processes (Bienkowski 1981, p. 262).

Notes

1   Following Frankel (1983) we use the words "country", "society" and "nation-state" in an interchangeable fashion.
2   We are not interested here in the question of whether these countries "really are socialist" (as in Fenichel & Khan 1981 or Gottheil 1981): this seems to us a fruitless quest to embark on.

3 The diplomatic representation at the unveiling of the new Republic of Bourkina Fasso in August 1984 was almost a roll-call of the socialist Third World:

> North Korea and Ethiopia sent their chief of defence staff. Angola sent its foreign minister. The Arab Saharan Republic (Polisario) sent its defence minister. France, Cuba, Algeria, Benin, Mali, Togo and Sao Tome all sent ministers. Vietnam, the PLO and Albania were represented by ambassadors (Brittain 1984, p. 15).

The country has since been renamed Burkina Faso.

4 Problems of the existence and coverage of data plague all attempts to consider the "developing" socialist countries. These problems must not be underestimated. Most economic data consist of estimates, which is not surprising considering the lack of competent administrators or, indeed, of administrators at all. Most urban data are unreliable and because of different definitions of "urban" are difficult to use for cross-national comparative purposes, except in broad outline. Data on subjects like social composition of the population are usually indirect or non-existent.

5 These changes can be fast. For example, the Soviet Union seems to be displaying so little interest in the African frontline states that "early in 1983 the American government invited members of Pretoria's state security council to Washington in great secrecy to give them a briefing with the CIA on the Soviet threat to Africa – or rather, the lack of it" (*The Economist* 1983b, p. 27).

6 Marx, of course, had little idea of the extensiveness of the modern state, so that "dictatorship" meant something rather different for him than it now does for us. For him "dictatorship" meant the equivalent of the Greek or Roman dictator, who takes up the reins of power for a fixed period of time only, these reins being harnessed to a state limited to an army, police force and a small civil service.

7 Clearly this description of what constitutes civil society, which comes from Urry (1981), is rather different from that of Marx – for Marx *bürgerliche Gesellschaft*, following Hegel, simply referred to the emergence of a modern (bourgeois) economy and state.

8 This description of society has been strongly criticized by Frankel (1983) as artificial because, in practice, in any society activities take place that cannot be clearly and unambiguously assigned to any one sphere. Although Frankel's criticism has some force, it is difficult to see what the alternatives are. Certainly, his alternative simply replaces the "holy trinity" of state, economy and civil society with four new categories – electoral, production, credit and food-production processes – which because they cut across the category of state, economy and civil society are assumed to answer the criticism. In reality, they just move the boundaries of the assignment problem about.

9 Each society has what Giddens (1981) calls "time-space edges" with other societies.

10 There is a long and continuing debate in the literature, from Bukharin

onwards, as to whether the ruling élite in the Soviet Union in particular constitutes a "class" and, if so, on what factors its power rests. An excellent review is provided by Nove (1979, Ch. 12): "Is there a ruling class in the USSR?" See also Konrad and Szelenyi (1979). Needless to say, this is an unresolved issue!

11 In the socialist developing countries this class would generally be quite small.

12 There is an extensive debate on whether centrally planned or market socialism is preferable. See most recently, for example, Frankel (1983, 1985) and Nove (1983, 1985a,b).

13 Indeed, the idea of an intelligentsia on the road to class power has been extensively criticized (for example, by Cohen 1982).

14 Where these influences combine the result can be very powerful indeed and can, ironically, be harnessed to a socialist ideology as in the case of the struggle by the Eritrean People's Liberation Front within (socialist) Ethiopia (Firebrace 1984).

15 Many socialist Third World countries are, as a result of warfare, extraordinarily frail entities. For example:

> a secret report to President Mugabe by Zimbabwean intelligence early this year is believed to have argued that Pretoria could topple President Machel (of Mozambique) in 48 hours if it wanted to (*The Economist* 1983b, p. 20).

Very little work has been done connecting internal development strategies with external affairs, but see Foucher (1979, 1982, 1985) and Slater (1985).

3 The problems of characterizing urbanization in socialist developing countries

Given that the socialist developing countries have reasonably distinctive social and economic structures, then it becomes reasonable to ask how these structures have influenced their patterns and processes of urbanization. In this chapter we will assess the evidence for this proposition in the most general way. The first part of the chapter considers some of the available empirical evidence via a comparative study similar to that carried out in Chapter 2. The second part of the chapter is concerned with how this evidence can be theoretically situated.

The empirical characteristics of urbanization

There are obvious differences between the patterns and processes of urbanization in socialist as opposed to capitalist countries. Just two of the more important of these differences are: first, as in many capitalist countries the rate of urbanization may be rapid, but in contrast to the case in many capitalist countries the spatial distribution of urban population tends to be relatively more even, and secondly, there is a deliberate concatenation of national economic and urbanization policies (United Nations 1980, Renaud 1981, Rogers & Williamson 1982). However, there are also considerable variations in urbanization patterns, processes and policies *within* the socialist countries. Table 3.1 shows the urbanization characteristics of the socialist countries for which urban data are available, ranked, as in Chapter 2, by GNP *per capita*. Although there are obvious dangers in comparing urban data across countries, discernible patterns do emerge. The countries of the Soviet-influenced European bloc are by far the most urbanized. They also have the lowest annual growth rate of urban population, the greatest concentration of population in large cities and (with the exception of Romania and Bulgaria) low primacy figures. The middle income group (US $500–1999) are less urbanized but they have higher annual rates of growth of urban population and a greater degree of primacy. Finally, the low income countries are the least urbanized and have a low concentration of population in large cities, but they also have the highest annual rate of growth of urban population and a degree of primacy that is similar to that of the middle income countries.

Substituting the more complex Wiles grouping of Chapter 2, Table 3.2 presents the results of a very simple exercise in considering differences in urbanization trends among socialist countries. Given that the data cut across some revolutions, especially those of the more recently declared socialist countries, a strong pattern still emerges. Stable or decreasing rates of growth of urban population are characteristic of the core countries in Groups 1 and 2 and these are usually based upon low rates of growth to begin with. However, amongst the socialist developing countries and marginals of Groups 3 and 4, although there are few absolute increases, rates of growth of urban population are often consistently high.

Over the years, a considerable amount of attention has been given to patterns of urbanization in the socialist developed countries of Eastern Europe (e.g. most recently Andrusz 1979, French & Hamilton 1979, Musil 1980, Pallot & Shaw 1981, Musil & Rysavy 1983, Szelenyi 1983, Rev 1984). These studies form a valuable resource, particularly since it might be expected that the diverse experience of urban planning in these countries would be exported to other socialist countries under Soviet influence. The findings of these studies can be very briefly summarized. The Soviet strategy, one followed in various ways by most of the Eastern European countries, has been to "economize" on the costs of urbanization and block rural–urban migration. Both "indirect" and "direct" policies have been used. "Indirect" policies have included the promotion of labour-intensive agriculture and capital-intensive industry, the restriction of household demand for better urban services because there is no direct link between productivity and wages, and housing shortages. "Direct" policies have included the direction of industry, especially to new industrial centres away from the major urban centres, the control of land use, the promotion of small towns and

Table 3.1 Urbanization in selected socialist countries.

	Urban population as % total population		Average annual growth rate of urban population (%)		% urban population in largest city	
	1960	1980	1960–70	1970–80	1960	1980
Kampuchea	11	4	3.5	—	—	—
Laos	8	14	3.8	5.2	69	48
Ethiopia	6	14	6.5	5.4	30	37
Guinea-Bissau	—	20	—	—	—	—
Somalia	17	20	5.3	5.0	—	34
Burma	19	27	4.0	4.2	23	23
Afghanistan	8	15	5.4	5.8	33	17
Vietnam (North & South)	15	19	5.3	3.3	32	21
Mozambique	4	9	6.5	8.3	75	83
Tanzania	5	12	6.3	8.7	34	50
China	—	13	—	—	6	6
Guinea	10	20	6.2	6.1	37	80
Benin	10	14	5.3	3.7	—	63
Madagascar	11	18	5.4	4.3	44	36
Yemen, P.D.R.	28	37	3.5	3.8	61	49
Angola	10	21	5.1	5.7	44	64
mean*	11.6	18.1	5.0	5.3	43.8	46.5
Nicaragua	41	53	4.0	4.7	41	47
Congo	30	45	5.0	4.5	77	56
Mongolia	36	51	5.2	4.1	53	52
Albania	31	37	3.7	3.4	27	25
Korea, Democratic Republic of	40	60	5.1	4.4	15	12
Syria	37	50	4.8	5.1	35	33
Cuba	55	65	2.9	2.1	38	32
Algeria	30	44	3.5	5.7	27	12
Iraq	43	72	6.2	5.4	35	55
mean	38	53	4.5	4.4	39	36
Romania	32	50	3.4	2.9	22	17
Yugoslavia	28	42	3.2	2.9	11	10
Poland	48	57	1.8	1.7	17	45
Bulgaria	39	64	3.8	2.6	23	18
Hungary	40	54	1.7	2.1	45	37
USSR	49	62	2.7	1.8	6	4
Czechoslovakia	47	63	2.1	2.0	17	12
Germany, Democratic Republic of	72	77	0.1	0.3	9	9
Libya	23	52	8.0	8.3	57	64
mean†	44	58	2.3	2.0	21	17

* Excludes China and Guinea-Bissau.
† Excludes USSR and Libya.
Source: Renaud (1981), Szajkowski (1981), World Bank (1982).

% urban population in cities over 500 000		Major cities over 500 000		Two-city primacy index	Four-city primacy index
1960	1980	1960	1980	1976	1976
—	—	—	0	—	—
0	0	0	0	3.484	1.263
0	37	0	1	5.000	3.000
—	80	0	0	—	—
0	0	0	0	4.375	1.842
23	23	1	2	—	1.881
0	17	0	1	—	0.667
32	50	1	4	—	1.625
0	83	0	1	2.564	—
0	50	0	1	6.847	2.332
42	45	38	70	1.429	0.759
0	0	0	1	—	—
0	63	0	1	1.804	0.951
0	36	0	1	5.559	2.018
0	0	0	0	4.390	2.717
0	64	0	1	4.475	2.001
4.2	32.5	0	1	4.277	1.845
0	47	0	1	5.518	1.448
0	0	0	0	2.130	1.453
0	0	0	0	10.486	4.318
0	0	0	0	3.077	1.079
15	19	1	2	2.400	1.395
35	55	1	2	—	0.863
38	42	1	1	6.360	1.463
27	12	1	1	—	1.250
35	70	1	3	—	1.987
17	22	0.5	1	4.892	1.760
22	17	1	1	6.725	2.448
11	23	1	3	1.318	0.669
41	47	5	8	1.872	0.687
23	18	1	1	3.216	1.290
45	37	1	1	10.145	3.376
21	33	25	50	1.767	0.968
17	12	1	1	3.236	1.135
14	17	2	3	1.891	0.798
0	64	0	1	1.375	0.656
25	24	2	3	4.057	1.486

Table 3.2 Recent urbanization trends in socialist countries. Rates of growth are given on the basis of difference in growth rate of urban population between 1960–70 and 1970–80: 0 = 0.5, stable; + = > 0.5, increase; − = < 0.5, decrease.

Group 1: full members of the CMEA

(a) European		(b) Non-European	
USSR	−	Cuba	−
Bulgaria	−	Mongolia	−
Czechoslovakia	0	Vietnam	−
Germany, D.R.	0		
Hungary	0		
Poland	0		
Romania	0		

Group 2: non-CMEA but socialist for a long time

Albania	0
China	0
Korea, D.R.	−
Yugoslavia	0

Group 3: socialist developing countries

Afghanistan	0
Angola	+
Kampuchea	−
Ethiopia	−
Laos	+
Mozambique	+
Yemen, P.D.R.	0

Group 4: "marginals"

(a) Avowed Marxist–Leninist		(b) One-party "socialist"	
Benin	−	Algeria	+
Congo	0	Burma	−
Somalia	0	Guinea	0
		Iraq	−
		Libya	0
		Madagascar	−
		Nicaragua	+
		Syria	+
		Tanzania	+

D.R., Democratic Republic; P.D.R., People's Democratic Republic.
Source: World Bank (1982).

the control of rural–urban migration, for example through the use of the Soviet *propiska* or internal passport system, first introduced in 1932. In the most general way, these policies have undoubtedly worked, but there have been considerable problems. For example, labour shortages in some of the cities (caused by their ageing demographic structure) have meant that more workers have had to be allowed in than was originally thought necessary. These labour shortages have also led to the phenomenon of long-distance commuting from rural areas into the cities to work in many Eastern European countries (for example, Poland and Hungary; see Demko & Fuchs 1977, Fallenbuchl 1977, Szelenyi 1981a,b). Again, urban planning has proved a formidable task. City planners, for example, find it difficult to prevent government ministries (which often have their own housing, services and concrete factories) from setting up industry in the cities:

> The lack of a clear division of authority within the hierarchical political and economic structure is seen by many to be a major problem. Thus the big industrial ministries are the objects of manifold complaints by city officials because of their ability to influence city development, especially in a negative manner. Hence, they are accused of failing to build housing and services they have contracted for, or to provide the necessary finance for them. They expand their activities to the detriment of many aspects of urban life and operate their housing and services inefficiently, but are jealous of their rights. They fail to locate plant in medium and small towns where industry is needed. They fail to inform city authorities of their plans, or to co-ordinate with them (Pallot & Shaw 1981, p. 249).

It is noticeable that the study of the patterns and processes of urbanization in the developing socialist countries, with much higher rates of both general and urban population growth than those found in the Soviet Union and Eastern European bloc, has been generally neglected.[1] The exceptions to this rule, of course, are China and Cuba.[2] In China and Cuba, the same kind of general policy imperatives are found as in the Soviet Union and Eastern Europe: to restrict the growth of the largest cities, to limit migration from rural to urban areas, to promote small and medium-sized towns, and so on. Although the Chinese and Soviet systems are often contrasted, much the same kind of general measures have been introduced in

China as in Russia, including economic decentralization, control of internal migration (from 1954–5 on), new towns, and so on. However, one major difference in recent history has been the movement, sometimes _forced_, of people (especially the young) back to the countryside in large numbers. This policy of population movement, which started in the 1950s, was enacted on a grand scale during the period of the Cultural Revolution. It has been estimated that between 1966 and 1977 up to 17 million (mainly younger) people left the cities for the countryside (Cell 1980, Farina 1980). Recently, the switch in emphasis from small, rural factories to larger factories and the move towards a more market-oriented economy has again put severe pressures on the larger Chinese cities (see Banerjee & Schenk 1984). In Cuba, there has been a similar emphasis on economic decentralization, on slowing down rural–urban migration, on the construction of new, small towns and on the mobilization of urban workers for agricultural work (especially at harvest time, although the policy has not proved to be a notable success). Strong attempts have been made to reduce the primacy of Havana, but these attempts have, to some extent, been contradicted by the need to locate some new industries in the capital city (Susman 1974, Barkin 1978, Gugler 1978, Slater 1982).

Theoretical characterization of urbanization

It is much remarked upon in the literature (e.g. by Konrad & Szelenyi 1977, Ofer 1977, Szelenyi 1981b) that socialist societies are "underurbanized": that is, compared with societies with a capitalist economy their rate of urban growth appears to fall behind the growth of their industrial population. Proletarianization of formerly agricultural workers is not followed by a correspondingly fast migration by these workers from rural areas to the towns and cities. The term "de-urbanization" has also been used quite frequently (e.g. Cell 1980) to describe the drastic drop in urban population in certain countries after the coming to power of a communist-led government.

Generally, the use of terms like "underurbanization" and "de-urbanization" has signified nothing more than a broad comparative description of what is happening within the urban realms of certain countries relative to the realms of other countries. However,

Murray and Szelenyi (1984) have tried to synthesize these descriptions into a formal model of urbanization in socialist societies. At different points in the history of such societies, it is suggested, different types of urbanization can be expected to occur which will correspond to the point of development of two closely connected tendencies that operate in the spheres of both the state and the economy. The first of these tendencies is the increasing degree of sophistication of the state's organization of production. The second tendency is the evolution of the class structure, with a state class gradually consolidating its hold on the reins of the economy and, in particular, wearing down the economic power of an actual or resurgent petty bourgeoisie. The working out of these tendencies explains what appears to be the innate "anti-urbanism" of many socialist societies. In effect, the state, in trying to bring all economic activity into public ownership (a process that necessarily involves the removal of the petty bourgeoisie), reduces the economic diversity of cities and therefore their chances for growth.[3] Murray and Szelenyi (1984) also suggest that this anti-urban bias will decline over time, partly in response to the degree to which the middle class has been eliminated and state power consolidated, and partly because of the gradual appearance of a new "socialist" petty bourgeoisie, made up of family work organizations and even small-scale private businesses. The result is that over time the rate of urbanization in socialist societies may be expected to speed up.

Murray and Szelenyi (1984) are able to identify five types of socialist urbanization, each of which "can be 'ranked' according to the intensity of their anti-urban bias" (Murray & Szelenyi 1984, p. 93). These types do not constitute a necessary historical progression: some will be bypassed; others may never be reached. Instead, which type is extant and how long that type continues to exist is contingent upon a whole series of historically specific factors.

These five types of socialist urbanization can be related to the three-stage model outlined in Chapter 2 in order to aid clarity of presentation (Table 3.3 & Fig. 3.1)

THE "REVOLUTIONARY" STAGE

In this stage, the revolution is followed by one of two courses of action. The first course is *de-urbanization*, a short sharp and drastic cut in urban population, the purpose of which is to destroy the urban

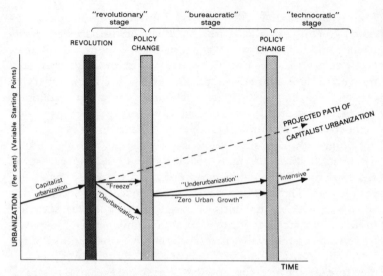

Figure 3.1 The Murray–Szelenyi model of socialist urbanization.

middle class and other opponents of the revolution (such as opposing armed forces). Understood in this sense, de-urbanization does not just consist of a decline in numbers – it also includes a change in the class composition of the city. Periods of de-urbanization like this can be found most recently in South Vietnam and in Cambodia.[4] The case of South Vietnam will be addressed in detail below.

Cambodia suffered a severe period of de-urbanization as a result of the Pol Pot régime coming to power in 1975. In 1945, the capital city of Phnom Penh held only 110 000 people. By 1970 the population had climbed to 600 000. By 1975, as a result of Cambodia's unwilling entry into the Second Indochina War, it held as many as 2 million people. Of this population, perhaps as many as 700 000 were refugees who had fled the war and were potentially mobile. However, the rest of the population of the city were forcibly dispersed into the countryside where they were made to take part in peasant agriculture, Marxist zealotry and vicious regional faction fighting. In all there were some 740 000 deaths in excess of normal between April 1975 and January 1979, when the Pol Pot régime finally collapsed. Of these deaths, about 300 000 were the result of execution; the rest were the result of hunger, exhaustion and illness. "De-urbanization" is surely too mild a term for this experience

Table 3.5 A simple model of socialist urbanization.

	Stage				
	"Revolutionary"		"Bureaucratic"		"Technocratic"(?)
	Type of urbanization				
	de-urbanization	freeze	zero urban growth	slow urban growth	socialist intensive urbanization
demographic characteristics	sharp decrease in urban population	some initial decrease in urban population	no, or little, change in urban population	slow to fast growth of urban population but *slower* than growth of industrial employment	growth of urban population but no drastic drop in rural population
mode of state control of economy	consolidation of state ownership of means of production		"organic" urban growth, emphasis on industrial development within the agricultural commune	"primitive socialist accumulation", accelerated industrialization at the expense of infrastructure and agriculture	intensive economic growth; more capital invested in economic development
class composition and conflict	struggle against the urban middle class with concessions to peasants; new cadres start to form state "class"		internal conflicts within the bureaucracy; state class, relatively few working class	hegemony of central redistributive power; state class and working class	emergence of a new petty bourgeoisie with concessions made by redistributive power; substantial working class

Source: adapted from Murray & Szelenyi (1984), p. 104.

(Kiernan & Chantou 1982, Chandler & Kiernan 1983, Shawcross 1984, Vickery 1984, Kiernan 1985)!

This kind of drastic de-urbanization needs to be fairly carefully separated from the numerous *population movements* out of the cities which often follow a revolution at periodic intervals, and which can even flow over into the "bureaucratic" stage. These movements can be composed of young draftees into the countryside, as in the case of China, or the "unemployed", as in the case of Mozambique recently (see *The Guardian* 1983, p. 3; 1984, p. 10). (Of course such a separation can sometimes be rather difficult to make since the "unemployed" are often former members of the middle class, left without a job.)

Periods of drastic de-urbanization such as those found in South Vietnam and Cambodia are probably fairly rare in socialist countries and seem to be restricted to socialist developing countries of a particular type: that is, those with a heavily primate settlement structure where the largest city has been swollen by war and reliance upon a colonial economy.[5] In many other socialist countries a second course of action is followed: a brief *"freeze"* combined with some forced dislocation of the urban middle class as, for example, in the case of Hungary in the early 1950s or Cuba in the first five years following the revolution.

THE "BUREAUCRATIC" STAGE

After the "revolutionary" stage has ended there follows the problem of how to achieve "socialist" urban goals over the longer term. Historically, two alternative routes have been taken. The first, the Chinese model from 1958 to 1975, is based upon (generally small-scale, commune-based) industrial growth *without* urban growth, partly because such industry is located in rural communes and partly because internal conflicts within the bureaucracy hinder centralized planning (see Cell 1980, Banerjee & Schenk 1984). This route produces what Murray and Szelenyi (1984) call "very slow" or *zero urban growth*. The rate of urbanization is slow or non-existent (although absolute increases in urban population still occur because of overall population growth). A similar pattern can apparently be found in Albania since 1965 (see Murray & Szelenyi 1984).

The Russian model produces what Murray and Szelenyi (1984) call, rather misleadingly, "underurbanization",[6] which we will call instead *slow urban growth*. Here, urban growth is slower than the growth of industrial employment. In effect, there is a "lag" in urban growth, which is the result of policies aimed at maximizing urban industrial growth (so-called "primitive socialist accumulation"[7]) while at the same time failing to provide enough urban infrastructure to house all the workers in the industry. These policies have effects such as the previously remarked upon growth of forced commuting by an industrial working class into the city from rural areas (see Konrad & Szelenyi 1977, Ofer 1977, Szelenyi 1981a,b, 1983). In class terms the city becomes the reserve of the new state class, at the expense of the industrial working class, for scarce resources are concentrated in the city overwhelmingly to the benefit of the new state class which lives and works there.

THE "TECHNOCRATIC" STAGE

Finally, Murray and Szelenyi (1984), somewhat speculatively, distinguish a new type of socialist urbanization, *socialist intensive urbanization*, in which the rate of urbanization speeds up. So far only to be found in Hungary,[8] this pattern is the result of a "technocratic" stage economy (in which industrial employment is declining) moving towards a "multisectoral" system within which a state-owned and administered sector of production is complemented by a significant private sector. This sector produces a new petty commodity-producing middle class which begins to rival the state class.

It would, of course, be possible to see these different types of socialist urbanization as forming a sequence, either "forwards" to a more refined mode of market socialism, or "backwards" to capitalism with, in each case, the implicit anti-urbanism of the "revolutionary" and "bureaucratic" stage types being tempered. Although Murray and Szelenyi (1984) seem tempted by this thought, they ultimately (and wisely) distance themselves from it. Szelenyi's (1984, p. 10) own summary seems the most realistic conclusion to our outline of the model:

> These types are probably not stages properly speaking. There are countries which may move through all of them but others may bypass some of them, or may even enter them in unusual sequence. But we claim that all (five) types are uniquely "socialist"; they express the contradictions of the "socialist

mode of production" or socialist strategies of growth in different historical settings, in different epochs. A common feature of all these types (possibly including socialist intensive urbanisation) is that they produce less population concentration than could be expected under capitalism in similar stages of economic growth.

The approach that Murray and Szelenyi (1984) take is clearly very general and it is restricted to that proportion of urbanization which can be traced to the spheres of the state and the economy. Theirs is essentially a model in which the class forces backing the state vie for supremacy over the economy; plan and market are in continual conflict. The model therefore ignores other forces, and particularly those emanating from the sphere of civil society and from external relations (especially warfare). There is good reason to believe that, in socialist developing countries in particular, these latter forces can have important effects on the pattern and rate of urbanization. Certainly, in the case of Vietnam, they have proved extremely important at particular junctures.

However, bearing these caveats in mind, the Murray–Szelenyi model is still a definite achievement: before it, there was nothing. In the chapters that follow it is therefore used as a structure to facilitate the understanding of Vietnamese urbanization from 1954 to 1985.

Notes

1 See the comments by French and Hamilton (1979, p. 3).
2 Although countries like Vietnam and Cambodia are now receiving more attention, other countries like Burma and Guyana, and a number of the recently declared African socialist states such as Ethiopia remain without chronicles of their recent urbanization experiences (but see Sisaye 1983, Forbes & Thrift 1986).
3 It is a much remarked upon fact that most revolutions which have led to the establishment of socialist countries have taken place in (at the time of the revolution) countries with low levels of urbanization. Even in countries like Cuba or South Vietnam where, at the time of the revolution, highly urbanized centres existed, the base of the movement tended to be outside such areas and was usually founded on an alliance between a vanguard middle class intelligentsia and the peasantry rather than (with some exceptions like pre-revolutionary Russia) being predicated upon an (often all but non-existent) urban working class (see Lowy 1981). Szelenyi (1981a,b) and Murray and Szelenyi (1984) have recently argued that

one of the reasons for this state of affairs can be found in a direct link between the strength of an urban middle class (rather than working class) and capitalist urban growth (a point made by a number of other authors, for example Elliott & McCrone 1982). Indeed, Murray and Szelenyi (1982, p. 9) argue that:

> We might hesitate to accept that a settlement, even if it has a large population, can be regarded as *urban unless it has a large enough urban middle class*, petty bourgeoisie. This is often the problem with "peasant cities"; settlements which are inhabited only by agriculturalists and hence are often regarded as rural even when their population is sizeable. The same can be said of "industrial settlements", as it is questionable whether a large housing development built around a single mine or a factory represents a(n) . . . urban place. The diversity or heterogeneity of the occupational structure we require as a criterion of "urbanism" indirectly measures the presence of the urban petty bourgeoisie . . . True, urbanisation opens up the gates to proletarianisation but it is coupled with a simultaneous further development of the urban middle classes. Urbanisation therefore has more to do with "embourgoisement" than with proletarianisation. Proletarianisation is possible without urbanisation, but "embourgoisement" is not.

The strength of this middle class increases with the growth in urban population to the point where in most developed countries it can block a revolution. Exceptional circumstances include those found in post-1945 Germany and Czechoslovakia, when World War II, coupled with increased Soviet influence, caused the necessary disruption to allow socialist régimes to come to power.

4 We do not address in any detail in this book the case of mass migrations from countries that proclaim themselves socialist, prior to the proclamation. These kinds of population movement could be regarded as a distinct type of de-urbanization which, if not occurring under a socialist régime, is certainly a response to that régime.

Such movements can be all the more dramatic when mixed with ex-colonial exoduses. For example, in Angola the urban middle class left *en masse* in the years before independence with considerable effects upon the population of the capital city of Luanda (Ottaway & Ottaway 1981, O'Connor 1985). Numbers have only now been fully made up. The urban middle class in Angola was mainly white. The whites, many of whom settled there in the period from 1960 to 1974, took over not only most of the top managerial and technical positions but also most of the more menial jobs usually occupied by blacks or Indians in French and British colonies (for example, as taxi drivers, fishermen, hotel maids, newspaper vendors and small shopkeepers). Three hundred thousand whites left in the year before independence. Similar population movements can be seen in the case of Vietnam.

5 To underline this point, no African socialist country seems to have endured a period of de-urbanization (O'Connor, personal communication).

6 Thus it is possible to ask quite legitimately: "underurbanized in relation to what?"
7 In fact, research by Ellman (1975) suggests that the devotion to industrialization in the USSR has never been quite as extreme as most researchers (and indeed Russian ideologists) have made out. Thus much of the lag in urban growth in the USSR was the result of agriculture keeping its (comparatively important) place in the economy.
8 And possibly in Czechoslovakia as well (see Musil 1980).

4 *Vietnam*

The Socialist Republic of Vietnam (Cong Hoa Xa Hoi Chu Nghia Viet Nam) is 329 600 km^2 in area (Fig. 4.1), and is possessed of a long and sinuous 3000 km coastline. Mountains and hills cover around three-quarters of the country. Vietnam is essentially a tropical country with a humid monsoon climate divided into a cool, dry season and a hot, rainy season. However, because Vietnam lies in the South East Asian intertropical monsoon zone, the north of the country above the 18th parallel experiences a cold winter as polar air blows south. In addition, the monsoon brings with it a strong expansion of the air to the north, making for much higher rainfall in many parts of the country than might be expected given the latitudes (Table 4.1). In general, Vietnam's natural environment is tropical in the north and subtropical in the south. However, the abundance of mountainous highlands means that a considerable area of the country has a temperate climate suitable for the cultivation of subtropical and temperate plants (Vu Tu Lap 1977).

Table 4.1 Indicators of Vietnam's climatic régime.

Location	Annual rainfall (mm)	Mean annual temperature (°C)	Mean annual variation (°C)
Hanoi	1678	23.4	—
Hue	2890	25.1	—
Da Nang	—	25.4	7.8
Qui Nhon	—	26.4	6.8
Nha Trang	—	26.4	4.2
Dalat*	—	19.1	3.4
Ho Chi Minh City	1979	26.9	3.1

*1500 m altitude.
Source: Vu Tu Lap (1977).

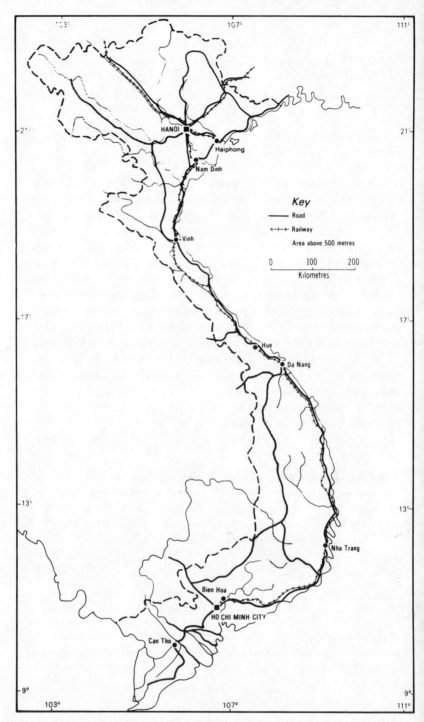

Figure 4.1 The Socialist Republic of Vietnam.

Table 4.2 Land disposition in the Socialist Republic of Vietnam, 1979.

Category	Area (million ha)		Percentage of total land area	
agriculture	8.4		25.0	
rice (paddy and upland)		5.5		17.0
other cereals (maize, etc.)		1.4		4.0
other foods		1.0		3.0
annual industrial crops		0.3		1.0
rubber		0.1		0.0
other perennial industrial crops		0.1		0.0
savanna and pasture	2.0		6.0	
forest*	22.0		67.0	
inland		21.4		65.0
coastal		0.6		2.0
miscellaneous land	0.3		1.0	
inland waters	0.4		1.0	
pisciculture		0.1		0.25
other		0.3		0.75
Total†	33.1		100.0	

* The forest category includes 2.1 million ha of lands not at present covered by trees (14% of forest category and 9% of all Vietnam). It also includes 11.1 million ha of commercial forest.
† North Vietnam, 15.8 million ha (48%); South Vietnam, 17.3 million ha (52%).
Source: Westing (1983), p. 366.

Only about 25% of Vietnam is under direct cultivation (Table 4.2) The bulk of the cultivated area consists of the "rice bowls" of the Red River Delta in the north and the Mekong Delta in the south. These areas provide the vast majority of the food for the population. Other cultivated areas include the coastal zones and parts of the Central Highlands. The coastal zones are notoriously susceptible to typhoon damage, and fishing is an important alternate activity. Cash crops like coffee, tea and vegetables are grown in parts of the Central Highlands, and rubber is grown in some of the lower areas of the south. Forests cover more than half of the area of Vietnam (Socialist Republic of Vietnam 1980) and forestry has become increasingly important in recent years.

The geology of Vietnam is complex and has provided a number of important mineral deposits, most especially coal and anthracite but also lignite and apatite (phosphate), iron ore, bauxite and, possibly, considerable reserves of offshore oil and natural gas[1] (*Far Eastern Economic Review* 1983a, 1984, 1985).

History[2]

After many centuries of domination by China, in the tenth century the Chinese were driven out of the north of what is now Vietnam. Although Chinese incursions into the north continued for centuries to come[3] (and have not ceased yet), and although the Vietnamese rulers sometimes had to accept tributary status, from this time onwards the Chinese influence on Vietnamese history was reduced.[4]

An important feature of subsequent Vietnamese history has been the precedence of conflict (Hodgkin 1981, Thrift & Forbes 1983) which was partly a result of the expansion of the North Vietnamese state into the south with the consequent setting up of two rival dynasties in north and south, partly a consequence of periodic Chinese incursions and partly the result of peasant *jacqueries* against what were often despotic régimes.[5]

Until the period of French colonization, Vietnam, like most of its neighbours, was primarily an agricultural economy based upon cultivation of wet rice via irrigation schemes. The land-ownership system was essentially feudal, with the ruler (or rulers) owning all land which was then awarded to nobles and top officials. Most land-holdings were tilled by serfs, but there was also a class of freeholding peasants. The space economy consisted of a few cities and a mass of virtually self-sufficient and self-contained village communes.

Beginning in the 16th century, Vietnam came to the attention of the European powers. In 1535 the Portuguese founded a settlement 24 km south of what is now Da Nang. The settlement never prospered and it was ultimately the French who made significant inroads into Vietnam. In particular, their influence was the result of the Catholic Church which, from the 17th century onwards, flourished in Vietnam, even though it was sometimes subject to persecution. However, it was not until the 19th century that the French became seriously interested in colonizing Vietnam, and the process of colonization was, on the whole, a rather haphazard affair being made up of equal parts official policy and individual initiatives. In 1862, three provinces in the south of the country were seized. In 1867 the remainder of the south was annexed and transformed into the French colony of Cochin China. Finally, in the mid-1880s the French completed their conquest of Vietnam, forming the colonies of Annam (Central Vietnam) and Tonkin (North Vietnam). The French had their "balcony on the Pacific".

The French régime in Vietnam is generally acknowledged to have been one of the more brutal colonial operations. In the early years of colonization a whole battery of measures passed by the colonial administrators, from expropriation of land for French colonists through the harsh working conditions on some plantations to the use of forced labour, made conditions difficult for many Vietnamese. In later years, the uglier side of French colonization was partly amelio-rated by attempts at democratization, including the introduction of some semblance of schooling and the like. However, the impact of these improvements was mainly felt in urban areas. In rural areas the increasing importance of the cash economy (which brought greater land concentration and rural tenancy) (Popkin 1979) combined with the world depression of the 1930s to produce considerable extra impoverishment.

Even so, the French presence did mean the bringing into culti-vation of large amounts of new land as well as the introduction of a number of export cash crops such as coffee, tea and, most especially, rubber. Greater use was also made of Vietnam's mineral resources, especially coal. In addition, the French presence meant the develop-ment of a number of Vietnamese cities:

> In the big cities of Hanoi, Haiphong, Saigon and Da Nang, as well as in smaller provincial capitals and market towns like Vinh, Nam Dinh, and Qui Nhon in the Centre and My Tho and Can Tho in the Mekong Delta, a young and vigorous commer-cial and manufacturing sector gradually emerged. Most of this activity was in the area of light industry: textiles, paper, sugar, matches, bicycle assembly and food processing (Duiker 1983, p. 31).

At first, resistance to the French was disorganized and sporadic, partly because of the growth of a new (mainly urban) class of Vietnamese tied to the French presence, including members of the colonial bureaucracy, economic middlemen, various professionals (from lawyers to school teachers) and a small group of petty bourgeois, who acted as a brake on nationalist aspirations. However, ironically, it was also out of this new urban class that the first stirrings of modern Vietnamese nationalism could be felt (Marr 1971, 1981). Nevertheless, it was not until the peasants and the new Vietnamese industrial proletariat took up the nationalist cause in the 1920s that serious resistance to French rule coalesced.

It was in these conditions that the Vietnamese Communist Party, led by Ho Chi Minh, took root and grew. After the unsuccessful 1930 Nghe-Tinh uprisings (Thrift & Forbes 1983) the Communist Party was quiescent for a number of years, but the Japanese occupation of Vietnam during World War II gave it its chance. Operating from within the broad front Vietnam Independence League (Viet Nam Doc Lap Dong Minh or Viet Minh), the Communist Party was able to seize power in North and Central Vietnam at the conclusion of World War II and proclaim a Democratic Republic, with Hanoi as its capital, on September 2, 1945. In South Vietnam, the French were re-installed by the British expeditionary forces. So, within three months of the end of the war, Vietnam had already been divided into a communist North and a French South.

However, by the end of 1946, after some bitter fighting in Hanoi, the North – or at least its cities and the less remote areas – was back in French hands. Meanwhile the Viet Minh regrouped: the First Indochina War had begun. The war culminated in the fall of Dien Bien Phu to the Viet Minh in 1953. That defeat persuaded the French, already looking for a negotiated settlement, to agree to split Vietnam into two zones, divided at the 17th parallel, by the Geneva Agreement of July 20, 1954. The agreement also called for free elections to be held throughout Vietnam in 1956. However, in 1955 the Southern government removed this clause and the elections were never held. Instead, once again, Vietnam was divided, giving a communist North (to be known as the Democratic Republic of Vietnam) under the leadership of Ho Chi Minh. The First Indochina War was over, at a cost of the lives of 520 000 North Vietnamese soldiers and civilians (Nguyen Duc Nhuan 1984b).

The non-communist South now made its own way under the régime of Ngo Dinh Diem, assisted by US advisers and aid. Diem set about some limited land reforms, but the promise of the early years soon slipped away and the alienation of the population was increased by the régime's fear of any opposition and its "agroville" programme which forced peasants to live in secure rural small towns (Forbes & Thrift 1986b). The opposition was, it should be said, quite formidable, and serves to illustrate Vietnam's considerable ethnic and religious diversity:

> Southerners resented alleged domination over society by Northern and central Vietnamese; the sects and the mountain minorities resented Saigon's efforts to place their areas under the administrative control of the central government; the overseas Chinese resented attempts to compel them to adopt Vietnamese citizenship; Saigon intellectuals disapproved of the régime's suppression of free speech; peasants were antagonized by the false promises of the land reform program; and Buddhists resented Diem's policy of favouring the nation's minority Catholic population (Duiker 1983, pp. 52–3).

The discontent with the Diem régime was sufficient to persuade the Democratic Republic to support the communist elements in the South, even though these elements had been extremely effectively suppressed. The National Front for the Liberation of Vietnam (NLF) was formed in the winter of 1960–1 on the same general principles as the Viet Minh. However, at about the same time the newly elected President Kennedy decided to take a tough stand on Vietnam. Thus the Second Indochina War began.

A crucial element in the Kennedy strategy for Vietnam was that conventional war should be supplemented by a counter-insurgency programme, the linchpin of which was the so-called "strategic hamlet" – essentially a fortified village able to keep communists at bay (Forbes & Thrift 1986b). Another element of the strategy was the replacement of Diem. In 1963, a *coup d'état* brought General Duong Van "Big" Minh to power. Unfortunately, this change of government was interpreted by the Democratic Republic as a sign of weakness and persuaded it to intervene openly. In 1964 units of the People's Army of Vietnam (PAVN) moved into the South. Thus both the US and the Democratic Republic increased their involvement at about the same time, and from this point on that involvement spiralled upwards in a series of moves and counter-moves. In 1964, for example, the US answered the Democratic Republic move and worries about the take-over of Southern rural areas by communist elements with the bombing of Northern military installations and then, in 1965, Northern cities.

In early 1965 a new régime headed by General Nguyen Cao Ky and General Nguyen Van Thieu came to power in the South. The new régime began to stabilize the situation, helped by the fact that the US had become heavily committed to the cause of the South under President Johnson. The PAVN had to take heavy losses in the hope of maximizing US casualties and thereby influencing US public opinion against the war. At the same time NLF operations in the South were affected by counter-insurgency programmes which culminated later in what is now agreed to have been the extremely successful (and extremely ruthless) Operation Phoenix.

The Tet offensive of 1968 changed all this. Approximately 80 000 North Vietnamese troops took part in an assault on the South, attacking major cities, provincial and district capitals; and villages. Militarily, the offensive was not as successful as has been claimed; by 1969, the year in which Ho Chi Minh died, most of the areas lost to the North had been regained. Nevertheless, the offensive was ideologically successful in that it persuaded the US that total victory against the North was not worth the cost in American lives. From this point on the US pursued a negotiated settlement and the rundown of US troops in Vietnam. The war was gradually handed back to the South to pursue. Peace talks between the US and the Democratic Republic, helped along by the stick of bombing and the carrot of bombing halts, now became a regular feature of the Vietnamese conflict until bombing of the North finally ceased in 1973.

In Easter 1972, a second offensive was launched by the North on the South which certainly contributed to the signing, in January 1973, of the Paris Agreement, which called for a ceasefire, the withdrawal of the remaining US troops and the setting up of a new "administrative structure" comprising communist, Thieu and neutral representatives. Of course, negotiations between the North and South broke down, but it was now only a matter of time for the South, especially given the US reluctance to commit its troops again. In early 1975, a new offensive was launched by the North and on April 30 NVA troops streamed into Saigon. The Second Indochina War was over, at enormous cost to Vietnam. About 1 million North Vietnamese soldiers and civilians had been killed and a further 1½ million were wounded. In the South, at least a further million soldiers and civilians were killed, and another million wounded (Nguyen Duc Nhuan 1984b). On July 2, 1976 the formal unification of Vietnam took place. The Socialist Republic of Vietnam was proclaimed with its capital at Hanoi.

Demography

By the end of the 1984, the Socialist Republic of Vietnam had a population of 57 372 000 (*Vietnam Courier* 1985), making it the world's 16th most populous nation. Average population density was 165 people per km^2, but in many parts of the country the population density was much greater than the average, most notably in the two most fertile areas, the Red River Delta in the north and the Mekong River Delta in the south (Fig. 4.2). These two areas contain 23% of Vietnam's land area but 57% of its population[6] (Jones & Fraser 1982).

Some 4.8% of the population belong to as many as 60 different ethnic minorities, especially Tay, Khmer, Thai, Muong, Nung, Meo and Dao (Table 4.3). In addition, there are a number of overseas Chinese. Although there were as many as 1½ million of the "Hoa" people in Vietnam as a whole in the middle of the present century, their present numbers are probably only three-quarters of a million (Shaplen 1985b). Minorities can also be religious. The Catholics form a distinct religious minority: there are as many as 3½ million of them (Shaplen 1985b). Two sects, the Cao-Dai (which appeared in 1925) and the Hoa-Hao (formed in 1919) also still exist in considerable numbers.

The Vietnamese population is growing at a rate of somewhere between 2.2 and 2.8% each year, which is high, although there is some evidence that this is slowing down (Table 4.4) (see Fraser 1981, 1985; Monnier 1981; *Far Eastern Economic Review* 1984; Nguyen Duc Nhuan 1984b). In practical terms, this growth rate means more than a million extra mouths to feed every year. It also means that the population is very young. In 1979, 44% of the population were under the age of 15 (Nguyen Duc Nhuan 1984b). In the same year 51.8% of the population was female and 48.2% was male (Fig. 4.3), but over time the number of males has been increasing.

Vietnam is now in a race to provide food for this rapidly growing, youthful population which may reach 76 000 000 by the year 2000

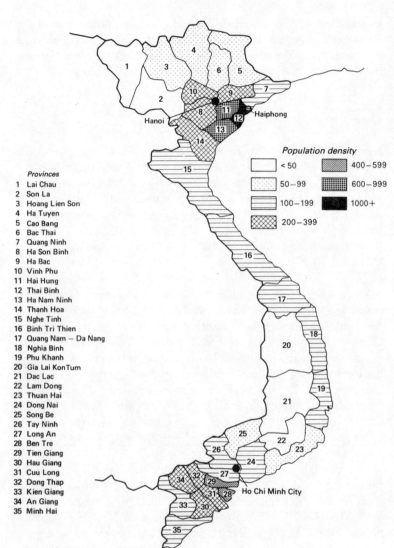

Figure 4.2 The population density of the provinces of the Socialist
Republic of Vietnam.

Source: Jones and Fraser (1982), p. 116.

according to UN estimates (United Nations Fund for Population
Activities 1981) and 80 million by Vietnamese estimates (*Far Eastern
Economic Review* 1984). Although self-sufficiency in food has now

Table 4.3 Numbers of ethnic minorities in the Socialist Republic of Vietnam, 1979.

Tay	742 000	Chure	8000
Khmer	651 000	Ha Nhi	8000
Thai	631 000	Sinh mam	8000
Muong	618 000	Lao	7000
Nung	472 900	Phu La	4000
Meo	349 000	Khang	4000
Dao	234 000	La Hu	3700
Gialai	163 000	Trang	3000
Ede	142 000	Lo	2500
Banar	78 000	LoLo	2200
Cham	65 000	Bru	2200
Coho	63 000	Lana	2000
Hre	57 000	May	1800
Sandiu	53 000	Chuc	1800
Sedang	53 000	Quy Chau (Pamuoi)	1700
M'nong	47 000	Pathen	1600
Cao Lan	42 000	Tu di	1000
Ray Glay	38 000	Co Lac	900
Stang	35 000	Ve	800
Van Kieu	29 000	Cong	700
Giay	26 000	Sre	400
Ca Tu	29 000	Boy	350
San chi	22 000	Sila	250
Ma	22 000	Tay Poong	170
Ta-oi	16 000	Odu	140
Co	18 000	Thuy	50
Khmu	15 000	Tong	50
Gie	12 000		

Source: Fraser (1981), p. 233.

been obtained, the country has to produce 400 000 tonnes more of food each year to keep the people supplied with their present minimal food rations (*Far Eastern Economic Review* 1985).

Economy

By any standards Vietnam is still a poor country. In 1983 its *per capita* GNP was certainly below that of China, although probably above that of Tanzania. Estimates of its overall 1983 GNP range from US $6 billion to US $16 billion (*Far Eastern Economic Review* 1985).

Table 4.4 Change in the annual birth and death rates of Vietnam, 1945–81 (per thousand).*

	Birth	Death	Overall annual growth rate
1945	37.5	24.2	13.3
1955–74			
North: 1955–60	46.0	12.0	34.0
1960–5	43.0	12.0	31.0
1965–74	42.0	14.0	28.0
South: 1955–67	42.0	12.0	30.0
1968–74	42.0	14.0	28.0
1976–81			
1976	39.5	7.5	32.0
1977	36.0	7.0	29.0
1978	31.4	7.1	24.3
1979	32.8	7.1	25.7
1980	29.3	7.0	22.3
1981	29.1	7.0	21.0

* For the period from 1976–1981 the birth and death rates are likely to be underestimates.
Source: Nguyen Duc Nhuan (1984b), p. 316.

The economy is dependent in two ways. First, it is dependent upon agriculture, which means that it is open to the vagaries of droughts, typhoons and floods. Secondly, it is dependent upon the Soviet bloc. In 1978 the Socialist Republic became a member of the CMEA and it is now almost entirely dependent upon the Soviet bloc for trade and aid. The value of imports is currently about four times the value of exports. Imports come mainly from the USSR and the Eastern European countries; Japan and India also figure prominently (Table 4.5). Chief amongst these imports are fuel, wheat, rice, petroleum products, steel, fertilizer, spare parts, and drugs and medicines. Exports are, again, mainly taken by the USSR and the Eastern European countries; Hong Kong also figures to a lesser extent (Table 4.5). Exports include seafood, handicrafts, footwear and, increasingly, rubber, tea and coffee. However, because of the reliance on the Soviet bloc only US $200 million worth of hard currency was generated in 1983 (Byrnes 1985b).

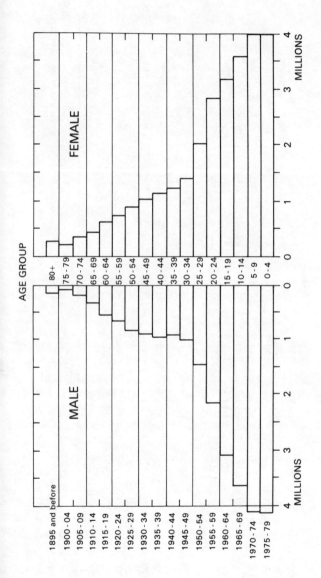

Figure 4.3 Approximate age pyramid for Vietnam, 1979.
Source: Nguyen Duc Nhuan (1984b), p. 317.

Table 4.5 Vietnam trade figures, 1977–83.

	Total	USSR	IMF total*	Japan	France	Sweden	Hong Kong	India	Singapore	Cambodia
								Trade figures (US $ millions)		
Imports										
1977	1044.10	372.0	672.1	159.7	48.0	37.5	58.7	7.5	28.5	
1978	1465.80	446.0	1019.4	239.8	109.9	65.5	32.8	63.3	44.9	
1979	1653.00	680.3	972.7	128.3	109.6	61.5	20.0	101.3	52.9	
1980	1696.50	700.1	996.4	124.9	66.0	56.0	33.3	143.6	54.4	
1981	1817.10	1006.4	810.7	120.1	88.2	24.8	29.9	143.7	79.0	
1982	1601.84‡	804.2†	636.8	101.4	25.7	23.9	65.5	129.2	38.2	
1983	1678.92‡	904.1†	594.0	131.3	35.7	12.7	60.9	116.3	99.5	
Exports										
1977	309.00	176.1	132.9	48.4	2.9		14.7		17.9	2.1
1978	406.70	22.5	184.2	46.6	4.1		18.8		13.0	2.5
1979	383.10	225.0	158.1	43.5	5.2		15.4		14.8	2.8
1980	401.50	242.4	159.1	44.4	4.5		20.2		16.3	3.2
1981	384.50	232.2	152.3	33.9	6.7		30.2		11.9	3.2
1982	447.70‡	206.5†	199.9	32.7	5.4		73.9		19.2	2.9
1983	498.78‡	234.9†	216.9	34.6	6.9		63.9		30.4	3.2

* The IMF total includes trade with non-socialist countries plus Hungary, Romania and Yugoslavia but not the USSR or the socialist countries of Albania, Bulgaria, East Germany, Czechoslovakia, Mongolia, North Korea and Poland. Current Vietnamese imports from these seven countries are estimated at US $150 million per year; Vietnamese exports to the seven are negligible.

† In roubles.

‡ Rouble portion based on an exchange rate of 1 rouble to US $1.20.

Source: Indochina Chronology (1984) 3(3), p. 28.

Vietnam's total debt (principal and interest) has now reached about US $6 billion. Of this amount US $2 billion is owed in hard currency to countries like Japan, Libya and Iraq; the other US $4 billion is owed in soft currencies to the Soviet bloc. Current arrears are probably about US $430 million, although some rescheduling has taken place. Hard currency foreign exchange reserves are estimated at US $16 million, enough for only a fortnight's basic purchases (*Far Eastern Economic Review* 1985, Shaplen 1985a). The current budget deficit is about 15%. The severe shortage of foreign exchange[7] means that there is a considerable black market in hard currency, even after an 855% devaluation of the dong against the US dollar in 1985. The official exchange rate for the dong is still below the black market exchange rate. Inflation is another problem: it has run at 50–60% over the last few years.

Vietnam therefore has heavy financial commitments. These commitments cannot be met out of taxes. Farmers are taxed at an average rate of 8% of their rice production; less fertile paddy is taxed at 4%. Other crops are not taxed. In the industrial sector, small entrepreneurs and workshops operating co-operatively or privately have 10 or 15% of their income taxed. Establishments deemed not socially necessary (such as restaurants) are taxed at punitive rates of 70%. There is no personal income tax (Shaplen 1985a). The Vietnamese state has tried other means of raising income such as bonds and a government-run lottery, but clearly there is a dramatic shortfall, even though the government collected four times as much revenue in 1983 as in 1981 (*Far Eastern Economic Review* 1985). Much of this shortfall has been met by aid, mainly from Russia and the Eastern European countries (Table 4.6). Vietnam regularly takes 10–20% of Russia's aid disbursements and 30–40% of Eastern European disbursements. Only Cuba does better. In turn, the Russians expect and get the use of military facilities at Da Nang and Cam Ranh Bay. An additional amount of aid is provided by some of the Organization for Economic Co-operation and Development (OECD) countries, most notably Sweden (Schnytzer 1982).

The agricultural sector of Vietnam is currently doing quite well, after some very hard times, although the prevalence of free market trade in the food produced has caused the state considerable problems. In particular, until 1985, state employees, party cadres, pensioners and others in similar positions were able to buy food at heavily subsidized prices to compensate them for low incomes.

Table 4.6 Aid to Vietnam, 1976–9.

	Aid (US $ millions)			
	1976	1977	1978	1979

(a) Net aid disbursements (gross disbursements minus amortization of aid to Vietnam)

USSR total	2457	2959	3687	—
to Cuba	1848 (75.2)*	2380 (80.4)	3030 (82.1)	—
to Vietnam	500 (20.3)	500 (16.8)	500 (13.5)	—
East European total	366	343	375	—
to Cuba	143 (39.0)	131 (38.2)	167 (44.5)	—
to Vietnam	142 (38.8)	142 (41.3)	142 (37.8)	—
OECD Development Assistance Committee total	38 001	41 842	60 031	63 458
to Cuba	371 (1.0)	79 (0.2)	211 (0.3)	32 (0.0)
to Vietnam	186 (0.5)	305 (0.7)	454 (0.7)	418 (0.6)
OPEC total	6761	12 660	13 394	14 384
to Cuba	—	—	—	10 (0.0)
to Vietnam	6 (0.0)	—	5 (0.0)	1 (0.0)

(b) Net public aid and private capital (commercial loans) disbursements to Vietnam

OECD bilateral	161.4 [87.1]†	257.6 [113.0]	297.3 [88.2]	311.8 [69.7]
OPEC bilateral	6.1	—	—	—
non-communist multilateral	18.6	47.6	161.2	106.7
USSR	500	500	500	—
rest of CMEA	142	142	142	—

* Figures in parentheses show disbursement as a percentage of the total aid provided by that source.
† Figures in square brackets show aid provided by Sweden.
Source: Wiles (1982).

Now, these subsidies are to end and incomes will be adjusted accordingly. The major problem remains the industrial sector (Ton That Thien 1983). Industrial production is running at 50% of capacity, mainly as a result of shortages of almost every kind of raw material, foreign-made spare parts and electricity. Even though there are plentiful reserves of many minerals, there are no resources for extracting them. Industrial workers are still relatively few in number – 3 million at most (Shaplen 1985a). Unemployment is probably somewhere between 15 and 20% and would be much greater but for the facts that the three years compulsory military service soaks up many youths and that there is a thriving informal economy.

The Vietnamese economy is therefore in a semi-permanent state of crisis as its vital statistics show (Table 4.7).

Administrative structure

Vietnam has the structure of a classical socialist state. The party, known as the Vietnamese Communist Party (VCP), is in command

Table 4.7 The economy of the Socialist Republic of Vietnam: some summary figures.

	1976	1977	1978	1979	1980
(a) Structure of labour force (%)					
productive sector	91.9	91.6	91.7	91.8	92.4
industry	10.1	9.8	9.6	9.4	11.2
construction	5.3	5.0	5.2	4.6	5.0
agriculture/forestry	68.7	69.1	69.3	70.2	68.7
trade and material supply	4.9	4.8	4.9	5.0	4.8
transport & communication	2.2	2.2	2.1	2.0	2.3
non-productive sectors	8.1	8.4	8.3	8.2	7.6
(b) Structure of "productive national income"(%)					
industry	24.3	27.6	28.7	27.6	26.8
construction	7.1	7.1	7.8	6.8	5.5
agriculture/forestry	48.6	40.1	39.3	41.3	44.1
trade & material supply	12.2	15.9	16.4	16.4	15.3
(c) Structure of imports (%)					
"means of production"	83.2	79.3	82.8	78.5	78.3
machinery and equipment	14.4	17.1	23.2	25.8	35.2
fuels and raw materials	53.6	48.2	44.6	33.5	30.4
consumer goods	16.8	20.7	17.2	21.5	21.7
(d) Structure of exports (%)					
industrial products	68.9	76.9	72.9	71.2	69.5
handicrafts	15.3	15.3	10.6	19.6	20.6
agricultural produce	15.8	7.8	8.5	9.2	9.9

Source: Socialist Republic of Vietnam (1981).

but government and army are also important. Despite the formal democratic aspects of the party's institutions, executive leadership effectively resides (at least between the party congresses which in theory are held every five years but, in practice, are convened on an *ad hoc* basis when important decisions have to be ratified) in what is currently a 15-person Political Bureau (13 voting members and two alternates) which meets twice a month, on average, and the 152-member Central Committee (116 full members and 36 alternates) which holds plenum meetings twice a year (Shaplen 1985a). Government is in the hands of a 486-member National Assembly elected every four years which, through a number of permanent councils, is linked into about 30 ministries (Fig. 4.4). Co-ordination between party and government operations is quite close mainly because of dual membership by party members of government organizations. The lines between party and the government are blurred, but the party assumes the dominant position (Shaplen 1985a, p. 116).

Of the 30 ministries, one of the most important is National Defence. This is hardly a surprise given the current size of the PAVN (which with a complement of about 1 million is one of the largest armies in the world).[8] Further, defence takes as much as 40% of Vietnam's GNP in any one year. The army is tied into both party and government. It is the chief source of party members and it has considerable influence on Vietnamese policy-making. For example, in 1984, 23 members of the Central Committee were from the armed forces (*Indochina Chronology* 1983, 2(4), pp. 16–17). Vietnam is not only a classical socialist state: it is also a classical militarized society.

The territorial administrative system of Vietnam is complex. The country is divided into 35 *provinces* (*tinh*) (Fig. 4.5) each run by a provincial People's Committee. The provinces are divided into from 4 to 12 *districts* (*huyen*)[9] (usually with a population of between 100 000 and 200 000) each with their own People's Committee. The district is (ideally) divided into *communes* (*xa*)[10] which are groups of *villages* (*thon*). A typical commune consists of 5000 people and takes in two to three villages. Finally, each village is divided into neighbourhoods known as *hamlets* (*xom*) (Elliott 1981, Fforde 1982).

In addition to the 35 provinces there are three *cities* or municipalities: Hanoi, Haiphong and Ho Chi Minh City.[11] Cities are divided into an "outer city" made up of *districts* (*huyen*) and an "inner city" made up of *precincts* (*quan*) (Figs 4.6 & 4.7) which are in turn divided

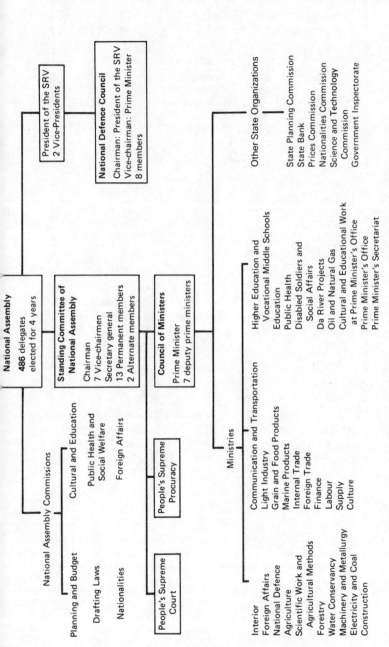

Figure 4.4 The government structure of the Socialist Republic of Vietnam.

Source: Elliott (1981), p. 728.

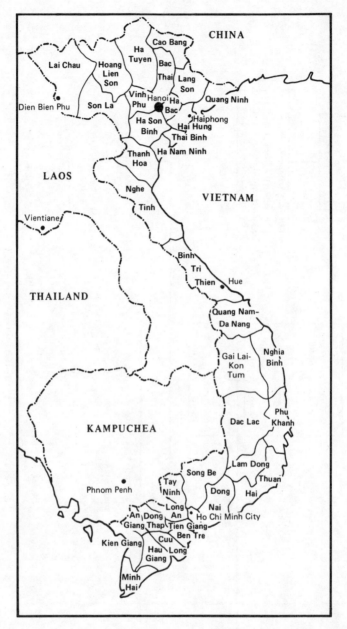

Figure 4.5 Provincial boundaries of the Socialist Republic of Vietnam.

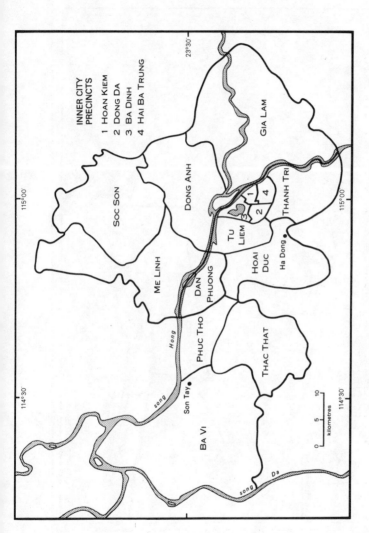

Figure 4.6 The administrative boundaries of Hanoi.

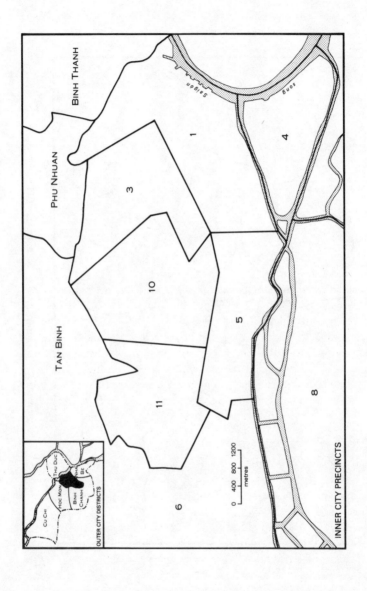

Figure 4.7 The administrative boundaries of Ho Chi Minh City.

into *wards* (*phuong*). The wards are usually divided into about ten *sectors* (*khu vuc*) or blocks. In turn, each sector is divided into 28–30 *neighbourhood solidarity cells* which ordinarily contain between 12 and 20 households. A city government is composed of a People's Council, elected by the people, which in turn elects an executive committee headed by a mayor. Under the executive committee there are a dozen departments in charge of specialized concerns like health, food, information, culture and education. Each of these departments gives directions to the executive committee of precincts on state policies and these are then transmitted down the line (Elliott 1981, Nguyen Van Canh 1983). In fact, the wards and their executive committees are responsible for most of the day-to-day running of the city.

This, then, is a brief description of the history and current demographic, economic and administrative structure of Vietnam. Other far more comprehensive synopses can be found in Elliott (1981), Schnytzer (1982), Duiker (1983) and, also, in the *Far Eastern Economic Review Asia Yearbook, Asian Survey, Southeast Asian Affairs, The Yearbook on International Communist Affairs* and the invaluable *Indochina Chronology*.

However, our chief interest is in the history of urbanization in socialist North Vietnam since 1954, when the Democratic Republic of Vietnam was formed (Ch. 6) and in the history of socialist North and South Vietnam since 1975–6, when the Second Indochina War ended and the Socialist Republic of Vietnam was declared (Ch. 8). This history is particularly interesting because it allows us to follow the course of urbanization of a socialist country over a long period of time in a number of different conditions (including warfare). In particular, it is possible to examine the course of urbanization in both the "revolutionary" and "bureaucratic" stages in the North whereas in the case of the South the exercise can be repeated but in what was (and still is) in many ways a quite different society with a distinctive historical and cultural background.

However, before either of these histories can be examined in detail, it is necessary to document the changes in the state, economy, civil society and external relations in North Vietnam since 1954 (in Ch. 5) and in both North and South Vietnam since 1975–6 (Ch. 7) in the most general terms in order to bring out their distinctive features. These accounts are *not* meant to be definitive statements;

rather they provide some of the necessary background on how a socialist state becomes determinant, a process which does not happen overnight and which is by no means inevitable. Many features of this process are themselves determinants of the course of urbanization in socialist Vietnam.

Notes

1 The Vietnamese are totally dependent upon the USSR for oil and oil products. Offshore oil deposits in the South China Sea have been explored for many years now but success has been limited, in particular because the Russians lack deep sea technology (Shaplen 1985a).

2 This brief history of Vietnam only extends to the point at which the North and South became socialist. Later history is to be found in Chapters 5 and 7. Detailed histories of Vietnam can be found in Hodgkin (1981), Duiker (1983) and Karnow (1983).

3 For example, in 1407 the Chinese brought Vietnam under their rule for a further 20 years.

4 Although clearly it still continued in, for example, the Confucian tradition of government and administration taken up by the Emperors (Woodside 1971a).

5 For example, the Tay Son rebellion which began in 1771 and resulted in the overthrow of the Emperor.

6 In the Red River Delta population densities of 250–850 persons per km^2 are as high as those of Java. In the Mekong Delta densities are lower (100–500 persons per km^2). Population density in the rest of Vietnam, outside the two delta regions, is still high by South East Asian standards. It is about the same as Thailand and higher than Malaysia (Jones & Fraser 1982), although obviously this density drops in the mountain areas.

7 Some foreign exchange is generated by the Vietnamese "guest workers" now employed in Eastern Europe and the USSR on two-year contracts. At the peak in 1983 there were about 50 000–60 000 such workers. About 16 000 of these were in the USSR (*Far Eastern Economic Review* 1984) and 14 000 were in Czechoslovakia, chiefly in glass and steel factories (*Indochina Chronology* 1983, 2(3), p. 5). Now, after a brief halt there are probably about 40 000 (*Indochina Chronology* 1985, 4(1), p. 6). Contrary to some of the stories that have been put around, these workers are not drafted. Instead our sources in Hanoi say that workers are desperate to go to the USSR and Eastern Europe – it is a way to escape the poverty of Vietnam.

8 The strength of the army is 1 000 000, that of the navy is 12 000 and that of the airforce is 15 000. These numbers do not include the air defence force, paramilitary forces or reserves (*Far Eastern Economic Review* 1985).

9 The district is now being strengthened as an administrative unit in line with the Fourth Party Congress resolution:

> Strong districts must be built; these should become agro-industrial economic units. The District must be the level for reorganising production, organising and reassigning the labourer to specific tasks, and uniting industry and agriculture, the economy of all the people and the collective economy, the workers and the peasants. The district level administration must be built into a state echelon that manages production, communications and life in the district (cited in Nguyen Van Canh 1983, p. 86).

10 Contrary to Chinese practice from 1950 to 1982 the commune is an *administrative* unit, quite distinct from the co-operative (Fforde 1982).

11 The inner city (see text) of Hanoi has four precincts – Ba Dinh, Hai Ba Trung, Dong Da and Hoan Kiem – all of which belonged to the old city of Hanoi. The outer city has four major surburban districts, two of which (Gia Lam and Dong Anh) came from the former Bac Ninh province and two (Tu Liem and Thanh Tri) from the former Ha Dong province. The inner city of Haiphong has three precincts (Hong Bang, Ngo Quyen and Le Chan) and the outer city has three main suburban districts (Ken An, Thuy Nguyen and Do Son). The inner city of Ho Chi Minh City has eight (numbered) precincts, and nine suburban districts have been taken from Gia Dinh province to form the outer city, namely Binh Thanh, Tan Binh, Phu Nhuan, Thu Duc, Nha Be, Go Vap, Hoc Mon, Cu Chi and Binh Chanh. The inner cities of the three cities are clearly made up of concentrated urban populations. The outer city or "suburbs" usually consist of food-producing areas for the city, with a more dispersed population but, in the case of Ho Chi Minh City in particular, there is a large urbanized population in many of the suburbs as well. This information is taken from recent maps and from Socialist Republic of Vietnam (1980).

5 The Democratic Republic of Vietnam, 1954–76: Building a Determinant State

The stages involved in the building of the socialist state that determined the economy and civil society of the Democratic Republic of Vietnam are summarized in Table 5.1 and outlined in the following sections. Many problems needed to be overcome amongst a population that in 1954 numbered about 13½ million. However, before commencing a critical survey, it is important to point out the extent of the changes the Democratic Republic was able to achieve. As Woodside (1976, p. 266) put it:

> this state, simply by its construction of a people's army, by its methods of manipulation, and by its attempting even the very decentralised pattern of industrialisation it has attempted, has introduced dramatic increases in the scale of human communication and relationships. On the part of the people who experienced these increases, normal reactions to sudden, unexpected expansions in the scale of human relationships may include efforts to reduce them again, in self defence, or to avoid their traumas – such as by self-isolation, or by quiet resistance to government interference. Hanoi seems determined to stay ahead of this phenomenon. To preserve all the new forms of organisation in Vietnamese life that it cherishes, the DRV government seeks not merely to control the expansion in scales of human relationships made necessary by its economic development dreams, but to manage and control their periodic contraction, as a necessary counter-point.

Table 5.1 State, economy and civil society in the Democratic Republic of Vietnam.

Sphere	Stage	
	Revolutionary	Bureaucratic
state	based on leadership of a few cadres and co-optation of old state apparatus; party membership drives a priority	party and government organized and governing
economy	industry and commerce nationalized; class struggle in countryside and confused aftermath	first Five Year Plan in place; swings from private to public in economy
civil society	fairly homogeneous; mass education instituted	mass education in place and functioning; women's programmes, etc.
class composition within state "class"	revolutionaries and cadres	ageing revolutionaries vs bureaucracy
other classes	small capitalist class destroyed; small industrial working class; peasantry are largest class	larger industrial working class
external relations	reliant on China and USSR	gradually becomes part of Soviet bloc; warfare

Initial conditions and ideological predispositions

From its inception, the builders of the socialist state were faced by numerous conflicting priorities, amongst which economic priorities stood out as the most pressing. Many of the problems of political integration were, as they have continued to be in the Socialist Republic, problems of economic development (Elliott 1976, 1981). Two major economic problems had to be faced immediately. First, the country lacked an industrial base. Although the French colonial authorities had been opposed to many forms of industrialization, still a relatively substantial set of manufacturing industries had grown up in the North during the 1930s (see Robequain 1944, Miller 1947, Murray 1980). However, by 1954 the war had severely reduced this industry, especially that operating on a large scale. Although Charrière (cited in Nyland 1981) probably exaggerated slightly when he stated that in 1954 the modern manufacturing sector consisted of just seven *large* enterprises (including a distillery, brewery and ice-making plant! (see Nguyen Tien Hung 1977)), still Le Duan's testimony (cited in Nyland 1981, p. 431) that in 1954, "we produced not a kilogram of steel or a kilogram of chemicals. Electricity sufficient only to light a few cities. Engineering comprised only small repair workshops . . ." is not so very far from the truth. Certainly, experience of manning industry was in very short supply.

The second major economic problem was a crisis in agriculture. In 1954 a good proportion of the people of North Vietnam lived near to starvation, the result of not enough food to satisfy the needs of the rapidly growing population. In the confused aftermath of World War II, for example, nearly 2 million people had died of starvation – 10% of the population. The deaths were concentrated in the Red River Delta. This was not surprising: already in 1936, the Red River Delta contained 32.6% of the total population of Indochina on only 2% of the land area. The population density of the Red River Delta was probably 430 people per km^2 in 1931, higher than Java's 315 per km^2 (Gourou 1940, 1965). Indeed, in some provinces the population density in 1921 already exceeded 1160 per km^2. By 1954 the Democratic Republic had the lowest *per capita* area of cultivated land in the world, yet 90% of the population depended on agriculture for their livelihood. Food shortages are endemic in the history of the Democratic Republic, and it is true to say that the birth rate meant that problems of food and population were "never far from the thoughts of North Vietnamese leaders" (Jones 1982, p. 783) (Table 5.2).

What was the response of the new régime to these twin problems of lack of industry and lack of food? This response requires some advance explanation of the constants in the underlying ideology of the Vietnamese Communist Party which persist to the present. Care must be taken to separate out some of the more transient (though none the less important) elements such as swings to and from "Maoist" thought. First, the practice of Vietnamese socialism has

Table 5.2 Estimates of the Democratic Republic of Vietnam food balance (million tons crude milled rice equivalent).

Year	Production	Estimate of net imports	Per capita availability per month (kg)
1960	3.0	>0.1	16
1965	3.6	>0.1	16
1965–75 (average)	3.8	0.5	15

Source: Fforde (1982), p. 50.

always taken place against the background of an intense *theoretical* debate. The Vietnamese revolution was led by a vanguard, primarily nationalist-oriented, intelligentsia which only gradually began to analyze the world in Marxist class terms (see, for example, Marr 1981, Huynh Kim Khanh 1982) and then base its policy on this analysis. This intelligentsia did not slide quickly or easily into orthodox Marxist–Leninism and, as a result, the Vietnamese Communist Party still retains some less orthodox elements and a certain amount of flexibility although still claiming "to be the most faithful followers of doctrine" (Boudarel 1980, p. 137).

Secondly, the *goals* of socialism are much the same in Vietnam as in many other socialist countries, that is, state ownership of the means of production, comprehensive planning of the economy, free provision of the basic necessities of life and the "dictatorship of the proletariat". The argument is over the *means*. In this context, it is important to note that the Vietnamese Communist Party did not at any time consider the Democratic Republic to be a fully fledged socialist society, as it now does not consider the Socialist Republic to be such a society. Le Duan's assessment (quoted in Nyland 1981, p. 426) is that, "We are building socialism, but a small scale basically agricultural economy still prevails. There are new relations of production but we cannot say that we have a socialist mode of production." Thus, the Vietnamese "road to socialism" has usually been characterized by a *relatively* pragmatic rather than a monolithic stance. As White (1982a, p. 24) puts it, "the preference in Vietnamese politics continues to be compromise and leaving options open, rather than polarised solutions, in contrast to China's style of swings from one policy extreme to the other".

Thirdly, all this said, certain *immutables* can be found in the

Vietnamese means of attaining socialism in the long run (White 1982a). These are fivefold:

(a) socialism means industrialization;

(b) industrialization means large-scale production in both industry and agriculture;

(c) the Communist Party must play the leading rôle;

(d) the market cannot provide basic human needs;

(e) the state must exist to guarantee the basic necessities of life.

Fourthly, Vietnamese socialism (like nearly all brands of socialism in socialist developing countries) is strongly tinged with an aggressive *nationalism* that has a long history of definition in struggle with outside forces to build a nation–state (see Hodgkin 1981, for the official account). It is based upon a mixture of socialist principles with local elements that go together to form a "kind of purified, demonetised Confucian tradition" (Woodside 1976, p. 266). Because of this history of struggle with outside forces, *external relations* have been a crucial element in the *internal* politics and policies of the Democratic Republic, and later of the Socialist Republic. As pointed out in Chapter 4 the history of Vietnam has always been intimately related to the history of China. Indeed, the very idea of Vietnam as a nation comes, at least in part, from a history of constant opposition to Chinese rule. A mistrust of China is therefore something of a constant in Vietnamese history (see, for example, Hodgkin 1981, Anderson 1983). However, the Vietnamese Communist Party was also, through its history, constantly helped by Chinese aid and sustenance, and a wing of the party that supported greater links with Beijing dominated until 1956. From 1956 there seems to have been a struggle for ascendancy within the party which appears to have been resolved in favour of elements who supported greater links with Moscow by, but not before, 1965.[1] The pattern of aid to some extent reflects these shifts of fortune. Thus the period from 1955 until 1965 sees a slow decline in the amount of aid given to the Democratic Republic by China (Fall 1967) and an increase in aid coming from the USSR. From 1965 to 1975 the USSR provided the Democratic Republic with US $1778 million in non-military aid (as against US $1491 million from China) and considerably more military aid than China. It seems reasonable to assume, then, that from 1965 onwards elements likely to be more sympathetic to Moscow, often on simple pragmatic grounds, including the current party General Secretary Le Duan (first appointed to the post in 1960) and the current Prime Minister, Pham Van Dong, gradually gained ascendancy within the party and slowly aligned North Vietnam with Moscow. Their position was only strengthened by the US bombing from 1964 to 1965 and the Cultural Revolution in China (see Schnytzer 1982). Of course, each step closer to Russia only served to alienate China further and increase the level of tension. Thus, initial neutrality in the face of the Sino-Soviet dispute in 1961 gradually became a commitment to Moscow. Already in 1967 Fall (1967, p. 199) could write, "The brutal truth is that for so small and exposed a country as North Viet-Nam, the number of policy choices is not infinite."

The ideology of the Vietnamese Communist Party is therefore adaptable – although within the limits set by its brand of socialism and nationalism. This means that it is still possible within the history of the Democratic Republic to see numerous ideological shifts within the party or factions of the party (see Zasloff & Brown 1975, Turley 1980b). However three ideological periods stand out (which are not necessarily reflected in the handling of the economy, for example). First, from 1954 to 1958 there was an initial, intensely ideological period. In the cities the emphasis was on the establishment of heavy industry. In the countryside class analysis and an active programme of class "struggle" were considered the keys to solving problems of rural development, the only difficulty being the general absence of any important national bourgeoisie to overcome. Attention therefore focused on the petty bourgeoisie and the rich peasants. The excesses of this programme produced increasing unrest, culminating in November 1956 in a rebellion in one of the heartlands of the revolution, the province of Nghe-An, which had to be put down by a whole division of the army (Fall 1967). Close to 6000 farmers may have been deported or executed (Moise 1976). This was a salutary shock for the party leadership. They had initiated a programme that they were subsequently unable to control. The programme, which had already been criticized by Ho Chi Minh, Vo Nguyen Giap and others, was brought to a halt. Secondly, the period from 1956 to 1965 can be seen as a period of struggle for hegemony within the party between pragmatists and idealists (combined with a need for leadership to re-assert control over both the party and the peasantry). Finally from 1965 onwards, with the onset of the Second Indochina War, the Democratic Republic became more orthodox in its brand of socialism and tilted strongly towards Moscow, a tendency not unconnected with the need for military aid.[2]

Advantages and disadvantages

The North Vietnamese "socialist" state was able to grow rapidly and, certainly by the standards of the developing countries, function relatively efficiently from an early date. It reached the "bureaucratic" stage early on, perhaps by the time of the publication of the first Five Year Plan (1960–5) in 1960, although the extent and effectiveness of the bureaucracy was of course severely curtailed by the typical conditions of scarcity and shortage facing all developing countries (Table 5.2). There were at least four reasons for this early crystallization of the state. First, the army and party were well integrated by the early 1950s and the party had a tight hold on the army (see Turley 1975a). Secondly, the existence of the so-called *hiérarchies parallèles* (parallel hierarchies), which Fall (1967, p. 133) has called "the true innovation of the (First) Indochina war", not only enabled a swift transition from one state to another to take place, but also allowed the "socialist" state to take control rapidly. These hierarchies were Viet Minh Administrative Units that, in effect, duplicated the French administration and which meant that already before the end of the war one state existed within the other. The parallel hierarchy was based upon a territorial division. Each village had its own administrative committee. This committee was answerable to a village group which was, in turn, part of a district. The district was part of a province and the province was part of a zone. The effect of this hierarchy is well described in a French army study of the time (cited in Fall 1967, p. 134):

> The Lien-Viet (organisation of Viet-Minh subsidiary groups) included youth groups, groups for mothers, farmers, workers, 'resistant' Catholics, war veterans, etc. It could just as well have included associations of flute players or bicycle racers; the important point was that no one escaped regimentation and that the normal (territorial hierarchy) was thus complemented by

another which watched the former and was in turn watched by it – both of them being watched in turn by the security services and the Party. The individual caught in the fine mesh of such a net has no chance whatsoever of preserving his independence.

Thirdly, both the party and the government inherited the so-called "mandarin" tradition of a bureaucratic élite based upon the Vietnamese version of the Chinese mandarinate (see Woodside 1971a, 1976; Nguyen Duc Nhuan 1982a). According to Woodside (1971b, p. 713) the "Vietnamese cooperative cadres and directors still have not entirely eluded their cultural ghost kinship with the Vietnamese bureaucratic elite of the past". There was, therefore, a reservoir of ready-trained bureaucrats to draw upon. Finally, the party had, of course, gained some very limited experience of government in 1945–6.

However, to balance this list of advantages there were also at least three disadvantages with which the embryonic state had to contend. First, as in most developing countries, the range of skills necessary to manage a modern industrial system was noticeably lacking. Thus:

> Until the first graduating class of 633 engineers left Hanoi Polytechnical Institute in December, 1961 the 12,000 textile workers at Nam Dinh had *no* engineers at all (the French had employed 47 engineers or supervisors), while the Hon-Gay coalmine complex was under the supervision of *two* technicians, where the French had used 150 engineers and supervisors to control the operations of 11,000 miners (Fall 1967, p. 139).

Secondly, the mandarin tradition had its disadvantages in governing a state based upon centralized planning and fixed quotas, for it was a tradition that emphasized moral wishes rather than the exact meeting of norms. It was found that:

> lower officials still may feel no grave cultural discomfort in qualifying orders of higher officials, and the demonstration of personal morality is still considered more important in some instances than literal-minded observances of written rules . . . the Hanoi government has found a new epithet for this legacy from the past. It is called 'average-ism' or 'the ideology of being average' (Woodside 1971b, p. 712).

Thirdly, a centrally planned economic system cannot be installed overnight. This is especially true of the effectively Soviet model of planning that was adopted by the Democratic Republic. In this model the state Planning Commission prepares development plans to be submitted to the Council of Ministers for approval (see Fig. 4.4). Development targets and strategies are determined by the party. Implementation of these targets is the responsibility of the various ministries which, in turn, assign specific targets to the various firms and farms (see Cao 1978, Limqueco & MacFarlane 1980). Such a model requires a degree of administrative integration which it is difficult for a developing country with limited manpower, control and information to implement. Be all this as it may, "the enormous expansion and intensification of organisational planning in the north since 1954 is a fact" (Woodside 1976, p. 257).

Towards a centrally planned economy

As already pointed out earlier in this chapter, the generally orthodox socialist ideology of the Vietnamese Communist Party puts great store on the establishment of heavy industry supported by state investment (which, incidentally, was wholly reliant on foreign aid and industrial profits during the period of the Democratic Republic agriculture contributed in no significant way). Industrial policy took two related forms. First, after 1954, the régime undertook a programme of strategic nationalization which drastically reduced private capitalist control in both the industrial and commercial sectors. The small number of factories inherited from the colonial period were moved into joint state–private ownership before becoming wholly state property. Nyland (1981, p. 43) reports that:

> All new secondary industry, after 1954, belonged to the state and these new enterprises soon came to dominate the industrial sector. Their output, in terms of production, but not including handicrafts, rose in value from 40 per cent of non-agricultural production in 1955 to 65 per cent in 1957 and to 90 per cent in 1960. By 1960 purely private industrial companies no longer existed.

Indeed, by the early 1960s, property under other than state ownership was confined to the artisanal and small-scale industry sector. Meanwhile by 1962 80% of trades had been re-organized, and state and co-operative institutions had become increasingly responsible for distribution. By about 1960, therefore, the state was the dominant owner in most sectors of the economy (Table 5.3).

Secondly, the régime expanded production, helped by foreign aid but hampered by shortages of electricity and raw materials (Table 5.4). The Three Year Plan (1958–60) had emphasized both agriculture and industry. However, with the forming of the first Five Year Plan (1960–5) in 1960 (which signifies the date at which the North Vietnamese state began to gain a degree of control over the economy) the emphasis moved to the production of steel and other heavy industries, and away from the development of lighter industries (see Fall 1967, Nguyen Tien Hung 1977, Nyland 1981): a "classical" socialist pattern. However, a considerable amount of investment was still made in "local" or "regional" industry, by which was meant mainly small firms and artisan workshops outside the major towns (Table 5.4). In 1962 this form of industry occupied 550 000 artisans (mainly in the co-operatives) and 40 000 workers, producing 63% of consumer goods and 43% of the means of production. The value of this "local" industry (including the artisan component) was 55% of total industrial production in 1972 (Nguyen Duc Nhuan 1977, 1978).

With the advent of US bombing and the abandonment of the projected second Five Year Plan this pattern of reliance on small-scale industry was, if anything, accentuated. The temporary plan of 1966–7 was designed to cope with the problems created by war. It necessarily promoted the creation of decentralized industries capable of satisfying the requirements of the surrounding areas with a minimum of outside supplies (Fall 1967), especially given the decision (borne of necessity) to postpone the construction of large industrial

Table 5.3 Percentage state ownership in five sectors, 1955 and 1959.

	1955	1959
industry	41.7	91.7
foreign commerce	77.0	100.0
interior commerce (wholesale)	28.1	89.0
interior commerce (retail)	20.3	80.4
commodities and transport	23.6	70.3

Source: Löwy (1981), p. 135.

Table 5.4 Industrial production in the Democratic Republic of Vietnam 1955–75.

Product	1955	1956	1957	1958	1959	1960	1962	1963	1964	1965	1968	1971	1972	1973	1975
electric power million kWh^{-1}	53	94	121	160	209	256	368	460	595	634	376	759	550	804	1320
coal (thousand tons)	642	1214	1085	1549	2202	2595	3500	3300	3600	4201	2401	3402	1699	2297	4644
apatite (thousand tons)	—	24	66	136	261	490	678	930	846	680	—	218	195	173	—
cement (thousand tons)	9	197	165	302	381	408	462	491	600	573	70	353	155	229	390
chromite (thousand tons)	—	1	4	6	7	19	33	31	29	32	—	—	—	—	—
water pumps (each)	—	—	—	—	—	—	1367	1966	2064	2524	2138	918	768	685	—
chemical fertilizer (thousand tons)	6	34	23	32	51	57	108	296	159	144	119	235	179	194	382
timber (thousand m^3)	362	457	439	459	770	753	941	992	1107	1085	722	866	752	693	—
paper (thousand tons)	1	2	2	3	4	5	15	17	20	24	9	19	11	12	—
cotton cloth (million m)	9	48	63	66	78	76	95	80	107	100	83	109	73	76	88
silk (million m)	—	2	4	7	6	6	7	10	13	—	—	—	—	—	—
sugar (thousand tons)	2	5	4	6	11	10	19	25	27	31	14	14	13	14	0
salt (thousand tons)	95	88	110	125	130	117	144	127	151	153	173	198	150	164	—
cigarettes (million packs)	3	12	15	30	66	73	95	105	109	134	134	175	164	220	—
soap (thousand tons)	1	2	3	3	4	5	6	6	7	8	4	4	5	6	—
bicycles (thousand tons)	—	—	—	6	13	27	39	60	78	85	86	62	61	61	—

Source: Nguyen Tien Hung (1977), p. 144.

plants and instead send troops to the South (Nguyen Tien Hung 1977). By the end of 1968 the share of local regional industry in production was constant or had slightly increased (although there was an absolute reduction in production due to the bombing). For example, 70% of consumer goods were produced by this sector and the value of this industry stood at 54% of total industrial production (Nguyen Duc Nhuan 1978). New tax regulations promulgated in 1966 even encouraged the formation of small industries of a family nature.

The shifts in agricultural development policy and patterns of agricultural production in the period of existence of the Democratic Republic have been extremely well documented (see Woodside 1971b, 1976; Elliott 1975; Moise 1976; White 1978, 1981, 1982a; Gordon 1981; Fforde 1982, 1983; Forbes & Thrift 1982; Duiker 1983; Houtart & Lemercinier 1984) and we will give only the briefest of summaries here. The period before the 1956 revolt was one in which class analysis and class struggle held sway in the countryside. The problem was perceived as "backward relations of production" and, in particular, the unequal distribution of land and the means of production which was seen to be a direct result of the extant rural class structure. The population was sorted into five "classes" (according to a Byzantine set of rules) ranging from landlord to rich peasant to middle peasant to poor peasant and so to agricultural worker. In many villages quotas of landlords and rich peasants were delivered to quite certain fates of imprisonment or death, and their land was redistributed. These excesses were followed by a new policy – the gradual formation of co-operatives – which began in 1958 and was finally completed in 1966, by which time 85% of peasant families belonged to "high-level" co-operatives (where all the means of production were co-operatively owned) and a further 10% to "low-level" co-operatives (where land and tools were collectively used but remained in private ownership, the owners receiving rent for their use). Land-ownership was gradually transferred from individuals to these co-operatives. However, it is not clear that improvements in agricultural policy necessarily followed this socialization of production[3] – agricultural production remained static or even declined until 1963, when a slow improvement in production *per capita* at last became apparent (Table 5.5).

With the beginnings of American bombing of the North in 1964 and more particularly in 1965, the co-operatives began to play a

Table 5.5 Agricultural production in the Democratic Republic of Vietnam, 1960–75.

	1960–5	1966–8	1969–72	1973–5
rice (million tons paddy)	4.34	4.04	4.34	4.91
potatoes (thousand tons)	752	1305	931	711
maize (thousand tons)	252	227	209	211
manioc (thousand tons)	732	797	671	682
water potatoes/taro (thousand tons)	—	168	137	112
water buffalo (thousand head)	1510	1640	1700	1770
cattle (thousand head)	790	750	700	650
pigs (thousand head)	4310	5120	5510	6440
horses (thousand head)	48	70	104	122
goats (thousand head)	75	118	135	140
poultry (millions)	24.8	28.0	30.5	34.8

Source: Fforde (1982), pp. 378–81.

more crucial rôle which continued until the end of the war. That rôle was one of local economic self-sufficiency. Of course, this does not mean there were no problems. As Nyland (1981, p. 435) puts it:

> The war drained off a large proportion of the young men from the cooperatives. Moreover, the hostilities necessitated the most skilled and politically conscious cadres having to be seconded for defensive work. This, in many cases, left control of the collective farms in the hands of less competent and socially conscious leaders who were less willing to make sacrifices for the common good.

Indeed, the party was soon forced by the need to maximize productivity to hand over some co-operative land to private families, to restore limited property rights and to allow individual peasants a far greater degree of freedom in how the output from the land was distributed (see Fforde 1982).

With the ending of the war the co-operatives began to be perceived as something of a two-edged sword:

> the limitations of the cooperative system as the basis for growth in economic productivity became increasingly apparent. Crop multiplications, after some initial success, levelled off. Crop

yields per acre increased, but the nutritional density (population per unit of cultivated land) rose even faster. Increased yields could be attributed in significant measure to intensification of labour inputs. While cooperativisation could be shown to have led to rises in *land* productivity, labour productivity actually declined (White 1982a, p. 16).

By the early 1970s a new policy had been introduced based on surveys of soil type and aimed at encouraging co-operatives to move towards crop specialization on the basis of regional comparative advantage. However, the policy proved difficult to implement (See Woodside 1971b, 1976; White 1981, 1982a).

Contradictions in the state's handling of the economy

Throughout the period from 1954 to 1976 the Democratic Republic was faced with three contradictions in its handling of the economy which it could not solve, contradictions that continued after unification and which seem to be common to a number of the socialist developing countries with actual or embryo centrally planned economies. First, there was a contradiction between the administrative capacity needed to run a centrally planned industrial economy and the level of resources that is necessary to achieve such an economy. The power to co-ordinate industry, its inputs and outputs, requires considerable resources. Vietnam's poverty made and makes this a difficult task. Events like paper shortages become critical barriers to administration. Secondly, there was and is a contradiction between a centrally planned economy, with the state at its heart, and the existence of a market economy, however rudimentary. Consistently throughout its history, the North Vietnamese state (and subsequently the Socialist Republic of Vietnam) has had to introduce incentives, expand the market and even re-introduce private property in order to raise productivity. At the same time these actions placed the existence of the state (and the state class) in question. As White (1982a, pp. 20–1) puts it:

> Any move . . . in the direction of replacing some of the reliance on direct political control with more use of economic levers and untying the unseen hand of the market was a direct threat to the interests of those central and local administrators and political

officials who spent their time communicating plan targets and exhorting the peasants to fulfil them.

and more precisely:

> In particular, cutting off bureaucratic controls by reducing the extensive role of planning and state control threatened to cut away some lucrative niches that influential local people had built for themselves by their control of politico-administrative links and of the account books.

Thus there was and is a constant see-sawing in economic policy typical of most non-capitalist economies (see Nuti 1979). Thirdly, and closely related to the first and second contradictions, there was and still is a contradiction between a centrally planned economy and the need for some level of decentralized decision-making. So with the end of the war in 1975 the co-operatives – whose local self-reliance had kept the nation intact – began to be perceived as a threat, as potentially resistant to central control and planning. Thus:

> whereas the priority of the 1960s was to build up cooperatives as basic and self-reliant political units in the countryside, by the late 1970s cadres were speaking of the need to 'break the autarky of the cooperatives' (White 1982a, p. 16).

The rise of the importance of the district is at least partly connected with this imperative.

Penetrating civil society

North Vietnamese civil society contained elements that were potentially resistant to the new state and the new state class: for example, Catholics, the overseas Chinese and the various ethnic minorities. In 1954 there were about 2 million Catholics in Vietnam. By some estimates some 600 000–650 000 of these moved South when the country was divided (Duiker 1983). In all, some 65% of the Catholic population of the North had left for the South either in 1945 or before the Democratic Republic was declared (Houtart & Lemercinier 1984). Those who remained were still allowed to practise their religion, but the activities of the Jesuits were curtailed and the number of parish priests allowed to be ordained was strictly limited.

In addition, the Catholic hierarchy was expected to co-operate with the state. In contrast to the treatment of the Catholics, many of the ethnic minorities were actively wooed. For example, they were given a special place in the constitution and limited self-government within "Autonomous Zones".

Probably the major tool for integrating civil society into the state was the educational system, which expanded rapidly under the Democratic Republic (see Woodside 1976) and at all levels (Socialist Republic of Vietnam 1979). School attendance in the "popular schools" was 592 095 in 1958. By 1965 it had risen to 2 816 760 (Fall 1967). By 1958 illiteracy was already considered, rather optimistically perhaps, to have been eliminated in ethnic Vietnamese under the age of 50 years (Nguyen Khac Vien 1971). These efforts were only bolstered by the markedly national cultural character of the revolution with its stress on literacy campaigns, respect for the past and adherence to the *quoc ngu* script (see Marr 1981), and by attempts to integrate Marxist–Leninist teaching with these cultural elements. A second major tool of integration was the spread of new elements of social mobilization and, in particular, militias, labour unions, youth organizations, factory social clubs and women's movements. These organizations were particularly important in socializing what were often raw and inexperienced peasants into industrialized life-styles and, in this way, they contributed directly to the mobilization of the economy. Finally, an important success, which did much (and rightly) to cement the loyalty of the population, was the growth of a proper health system. Diseases like malaria, trachoma, tuberculosis and leprosy were gradually eliminated. By 1970 North Vietnam had one physician for every 5454 people, and one assistant doctor for every 1093 people. In 1975 there were 444 hospitals and 595 state dispensaries with a total of 50 000 beds as well as 6000 commune health centres with another 45 000 beds (Socialist Republic of Vietnam, 1979).

However, elements of civil society remained resistant to overall change and the régime was forced to seek a certain amount of accommodation, often through incorporation. First, patriarchal relations persisted although women were meant to have an equal place in the revolution (see, for example, Boudarel 1970, Woodside 1976, Marr 1981, Werner 1981, White 1982b, Eisen 1985). In 1965, for example, the "three assumptions of duty" movement required women to participate more fully in the labour force, the family and defence of the country; women were meant to become equals in the service *and* management of the state. However, these assumptions were interpreted by some co-operatives as simply meaning that women should work longer hours in the rice fields. In addition, before the promulgation of new co-operative laws in 1969, women often received fewer "labour points" than male workers for the same task. As Woodside (1971b, p. 712) pointed out:

> The traditional age–sex hierarchies of the Vietnamese village have not been obliterated . . . Crop improvements, 'deep culti- vation' campaigns, and expanded forms of organisational colla- boration can all be accommodated by the villagers' habitual conceptions of propriety; radical role changes, especially at the symbolic and formal levels, are more disturbing.

Secondly, many features of the traditional Confucian family "survived . . ., in ideology if not in economics" (Woodside 1976, p. 265). Thus although definite changes in the structure of the family were achieved by the state, for example in the equalization of hus- bands and wives, and in the abolition of family property ownership, the traditional family remained more or less intact – in part because the social framework of "teeming relatives of the traditional Vietnamese lineage" (Woodside 1976, p. 265) was hard to disassem- ble, in part because of official ideology and in part because it was a useful secondary basis for popular mobilization.[4] Thirdly, village customs and traditions have not been entirely replaced. Some village traditions have actually been incorporated. For example, in many places old village communal houses were renamed as village "con- ference halls". In some villages, village elder ceremonies are still held, but paper certificates are handed out to the new elders from the representatives of the local provincial committee (women are now allowed to become formal certificate-carrying elders) (Woodside 1976).

External relations

A major element in the development of North Vietnam was, of course, the Second Indochina War. The strategy of the United States against the North involved heavy bombing and naval shelling in order systematically to destroy industry, transportation networks and all public buildings (Table 5.6). An estimated 3% of the population of the North were killed and many more were wounded.[5] Many cities, towns and villages were bombed. Nearly every road and railway bridge was destroyed by bombing. "Many hundreds of water conservancy works and irrigation dikes were destroyed. 200 000 hectares of agricultural land were put out of commission. 24 000 water buffalo were killed. Countless unexploded munitions remained at the end of the war, continuing to cause scores of casualties, many of them fatal" (Westing 1983, p. 370).

Clearly North Vietnam suffered severe disruptions as a result of the bombing. As mentioned above, the economy had to be decentralized with consequent effects on the level of production (Table 5.4). In certain areas agricultural production decreased markedly because of the bombing: rice production was particularly badly hit through damage to irrigation works. Private agricultural production had to be encouraged (Fforde 1982) which was a potential threat to the power of the state. Furthermore much of the state apparatus also had to be decentralized. In all, the Second Indochina War had severe effects on the economy and society of the Democratic Republic.

Table 5.6 War damage to Vietnam during the Second Indochina War.

	Munitions fired (million tons)	(kg/ha)	Herbicides sprayed (thousand m³)	(l/ha)	Land cleared (thousand ha)	[m²/ha]
North Vietnam	1.1	70	0	0	0	0
South Vietnam	10.2	590	72.4	4.2	325	190
Total	11.3	660	72.4	4.2	325	190

Source: Westing (1983), p. 369.

Notes

1 Some doubts should be recorded about analyzing the Vietnamese Communist Party in terms of a clash between pro-Moscow and pro-Beijing wings. The reality was undoubtedly more subtle. "Top party figures often found it convenient to favour Moscow or Peking according to the needs of the moment but, for most if not all party leaders dedication to the cause of Vietnamese unification and survival took precedence over loyalty to China or the Soviet Union" (Duiker 1983, p. 86). A more abiding schism seems to be the one between pragmatists and idealists or conservatives (often members of the army).

2 Although the Republic continued to receive Chinese military aid until 1975.

3 There are numerous reasons why agricultural performance was generally below that expected, including shortage of inputs like fertilizer, the confusion of responsibilities amongst ministries and other organs of the state and party apparatus and positions of authority being used for personal gain.

4 This problem is found in all socialist developing countries (see Croll 1979, Molyneux 1981, Werner 1981). Vietnam, to its credit, seems to have tried harder than many other countries to overcome it.

5 Throughout Vietnam as a whole there are at present some 360 000 disabled war victims of labouring age (both military and civilian) who currently receive government compensation. Of these, 140 000 are totally disabled. There are also 1.1 million children who have lost both parents (Westing 1983).

6 Urbanization in the Democratic Republic of Vietnam, 1954 to 1975–6

The particular historical combination of the state, the economy and civil society in the Democratic Republic outlined in the previous chapter forms the vital background to the pattern of North Vietnamese urbanization from 1954 to 1976, but this is not a structuralist analysis and there is no question that the pace and pattern of urbanization in the Democratic Republic can simply be "read off" from this combination. An analysis is required that not only takes into account the specific conditions of state, economy and civil society but also a number of other factors stemming from the particular form and style of management of the North Vietnamese urban system. Three of these factors were particularly important in 1954 (Turley 1975b). First, the starting point for urbanization under the new socialist state was very low indeed. Most of the towns and cities were small and consequently fairly easy to control (especially since some of the lessons of urban governance had started to be learnt in the 1945–6 period). Only Hanoi, the former capital of Tonkin, and Haiphong, the principal northern port, were cities of any significant size with any significant industrial workforce. Hanoi, for example, had a population of about 400 000 in 1954 (and this figure is a generous "agglomeration" total reached only by including all the people in the surrounding agricultural area in the population of the city). The Democratic Republic was predominantly an agricultural country with only about 7% urban population. Secondly, there had been a negotiated transfer of power with a period of months in which the population of North and South Vietnam could choose which zone to live in. Thus there was an orderly departure of the French and, more particularly, many of those who might have caused dissent – the upper classes, the military personnel, civil servants, Catholics and collaborators. In all, as many as 900 000 people may have left the North (Duiker 1983). This exodus meant that the cities were inhabited by persons more likely to be sympathetic or at least resigned to the new régime. Thirdly, the Vietnamese brand of communism has never been explicitly "anti-urban" as, for instance, Chinese doctrines often appear to be. Rather it is based on the parallel and co-ordinated development of town and countryside. As Woodside (1971b, p. 717) puts it:

> the concept of the coordinated development of the cities and villages has always been an article of faith of the Hanoi regime. Perhaps such a preoccupation finds its antecedents in the Viet Minh (and NLF) military doctrine that 'the villages and the cities advance together', a doctrine which Vietnamese Communist writers . . . explicitly contrast with the Maoist Chinese doctrine of the 'villages encircling the cities'.

Thus Vo Nguyen Giap coined the slogan, "The crucial front in our country cannot be the city but our Party does not underestimate the role of the city" (see also Turley 1977a, b; Boudarel 1980, p. 151; *Vietnam Courier* 1980, p. 9).

With these three factors borne in mind, the actual pattern of urbanization from 1954 to 1976 can be traced out. Inspection of Figure 6.1 shows that between 1954 and 1976, allowing for the very unusual circumstances pertaining during the period of the Second Indochina War, overall percentage urban population growth was very slow. However, as the data in Table 6.1 show, this slow percentage rate of growth conceals a quite significant absolute increase. In absolute terms, the urban population all but doubled.

In so far as it is possible to tell from the available figures and other evidence, there does not appear to have been any drastic period of *de-urbanization* during the "revolutionary" period. The absence of any sizeable urban middle class, both because of the size of the cities and the exodus to the South, would mean that this would not have been an imperative. (Instead, the state and the formative state class reserved most of its attacks for other class forces that *did* seem to threaten it, especially the landlords and "rich peasants".) At most, there may have been a brief *freeze* of the urban population, although the figures do not allow any certain interpretation to be made. Indeed, the available evidence suggests that the whole period from 1954 to 1965 was one of *slow urban growth*[1] in terms of the Murray–

Table 6.1 Urban population in North Vietnam, 1943–85.

Year	Total population of N. Vietnam	Urban population of N. Vietnam	Hanoi (agglomeration)	Hanoi (agglomeration) as % urban population	Hanoi (town) as % urban population	Two-city primacy index (agglomeration)	Two-city primacy index (town)
1942	12 550 000	—	—	—	—	—	—
1943*	12 789 183	c.500 000	119 737	23.9	—	1.8	—
1948–9	—	—	10 000?	—	—	—	—
1951	—	—	216 900	—	—	—	—
1952	—	—	273 732	—	—	1.9	0.9
1953	—	—	292 575	—	—	—	—
1954	—	—	380 000–400 000	—	—	—	—
1955	13 574 000	997 000	—	—	—	—	1.7
1957	14 526 000	1 230 000	—	—	—	—	—
1960*	16 100 000	1 570 000	643 576	40.1	26.4	3.5	2.3
1961	16 600 000	—	900 427†	—	—	—	—
1965	19 210 000	2 113 000	—	—	—	—	—
1967–8	19 850 000	—	400 000?	—	—	—	—
1970	21 900 000	1 840 000	710 000	38.6	—	2.4	—
April 1972	22 500 000	—	1 200 000	—	—	—	—
Dec. 1972	—	—	480 000	—	—	—	—
1974	23 787 000	2 616 000	1 378 335	52.6	28.1	—	—
1975	24 547 000	2 651 000	—	—	—	—	—
1976	24 944 000	3 008 500	1 443 500	48.0	—	1.2	—
1978	—	—	1 550 000	—	—	1.2	—
1979*	27 264 372§	3 448 213	2 570 905‡	74.5 (45.4)*	—	1.2	2.3
1984	—	—	2 674 400	—	22.4	—	—

*Year of census. All other figures based on estimates.

†In 1961 Hanoi's geographical boundaries were redrawn and the area controlled by the municipality increased threefold; 256 851 extra people were absorbed.

‡In January 1979 Hanoi's geographical boundaries were redrawn and the area controlled by the municipality quadrupled. One million extra people were absorbed.

§In 1979 new administrative boundaries were drawn and the North was redefined to include two former Southern provinces and an extra 52 792 people.

Sources: Burchett (1956), Ng Shui Meng (1974), Nguyen Thy (1974), Goodman & Franks (1975), Turley (1975b), Nguyen Duc Nhuan (1977, 1984b), Fraser (1981, 1985), Monnier (1981), *Vietnam Courier* (1982e, 1985).

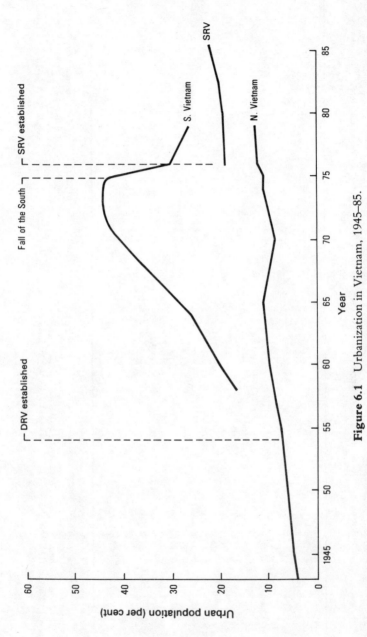

Figure 6.1 Urbanization in Vietnam, 1945–85.

Sources: Burchett (1956), Ng Shui Meng (1974), Nguyen Thy (1974), Goodman and Franks (1975), Turley (1975b), Nguyen Duc Nhuan (1977, 1984b), Fraser (1981, 1985), Monnier (1981), *Vietnam Courier* (1983, 1985).

Szelenyi model. The era of the war from 1965 to 1975 can be interpreted as a period of *zero urban growth* from 1965 to 1973 when the bombing was at its height, leading into a second period of *re-adjustment and slow urban growth* from 1973 onwards. What is our evidence for these interpretations? We will consider each of these periods in turn.

Slow urban growth, 1954–65

Our interpretation of the period from 1954 to 1965 as one of slow urban growth results from an inspection of the available figures and a consideration of the policies followed by the state likely to have had an effect on the rate of urbanization, especially the attempts by the state to direct the economy and the space economy in the integrated fashion that is typical of most socialist societies in a period when the problems of the economy are manifold and manifestly serious. In particular, the state followed an industrial policy (of the kind that classically leads to slow urban growth) that was bound to have effects on the North Vietnamese cities. Thus, when the French vacated Vietnam they left behind only the two major cities of Hanoi, the administrative city with its various consumer industries, and Haiphong, a port almost solely oriented to commerce with France (see Murray 1980). Attempts were therefore made to create a series of urban industrial centres. Thirteen in all were designated (Table 6.2). Seven were based on particular sources of energy and minerals (mainly funded from Soviet and Chinese aid). Six more, including Hanoi and Haiphong, were planned to have more diverse industrial bases, partly based upon extant industry (Nguyen Duc Nhuan 1977, 1978). Added to these primary centres were a series of small towns with one or two factories and then a sprawl of small village-based industries. Thus, a more even urban hierarchy was to be created which at the same time would support industrial growth.

The creation of this set of urban industrial centres must have had strongly centralizing effects. However, an urban population boom did not follow. Indeed, in so far as it is possible to tell from Table 6.3, the rate of increase in urban population lagged behind the rate of increase in industrial employment throughout the period, the classical indicator of slow urban growth. There were a number of reasons for this relative lack of urban growth, of which four stand

Table 6.2 Major industrial centres of the Democratic Republic of Vietnam.

Town or province	Products
(a) Diverse industrial centres	
Hanoi	consumer industries, machinery manufacture
Haiphong	port with port industries, machinery manufacture
Nam Dinh	diverse, including textiles and light industry complex
Van Dien	diverse
Thanh Hoa	diverse (includes apatite)
Vinh	diverse
(b) Energy and minerals centres	
Cao Bang	tin
Lao Cai	apatite, chlorides, sulphuric acid, insecticides, food processing, phosphates
Phu Tho	phosphates
Viet Tri/Lam Thao	chemicals complex (sugar cane refinery, antibiotics, paper)
Hon Gai	anthracite
Thai Nguyen	steel complex
Thac Ba	hydroelectric complex

Sources: Fall (1967). Nguyen Duc Nhuan (1978).

Table 6.3 Industrialization and urbanization in the Democratic Republic of Vietnam.

	1945	1955	1960	1965	1970
urban population as % of total population	4.9	7.4	9.6	10.8	9.8
industrial employment as % of total employment	—	18.2	25.7	27.6	—

Source: Nguyen Thy (1974).

out, apart from the fact that the policy was of course explicitly designed to "even out" and slow down the effects of urban growth. First, the success of the industrial policy was made problematic by scarcities and shortages – not as much industry resulted as was first envisaged. Secondly, the infrastructural investments needed to support an urban population based upon this industrial policy (especially housing) were not made. Thirdly, there were some limited attempts to discourage migration to the larger cities.[2] As Nguyen Duc Nhuan (1978, p. 346) puts it:

c'est grâce à de tels résultats de l'industrialisation régionale et locale que le Viet Nam du Nord a pu éviter le processus d'exode rural et de la constitution des grands bidonvilles si tristement suivi pars les autres pays du tiers monde engagé dans la voie capitaliste du développement.

Fourthly, the seriousness of the effects of the demographic situation upon food supplies, especially the effects of a population growth rate which varied between 2 and 3% per annum, led to the need to cut the population growth rate and boost agricultural production. There were, of course, a number of events that naturally alleviated this population growth – for example, there was the exodus of 900 000 refugees to the South, and the execution of many North Vietnamese (estimates vary from 4400 to as many as 50 000) in the period of "class struggle in the countryside" (see Fall 1967 and Moise 1976 for conflicting accounts) – however, inevitably large-scale demographic policies had to be set in place. These were twofold. First, birth control programmes were set up in 1963 (see United Nations Fund for Population Activities 1978; Fraser 1979, 1985; Jones 1982; Nguyen Duc Nhuan 1984b). These had a limited effect (see Table 4.4). Secondly, commencing with the 1961–5 Five Year Plan, population resettlement programmes were devised with two main motivations: to reduce the high population densities in the North, especially in the Red River Delta, and to spread the population more evenly over the countryside and thus bring into cultivation previously unworked areas. From 1961 to 1975 approximately 1 million people were persuaded to leave the Red River Delta provinces and settle in "New Economic Zones" in the sparsely populated upland provinces of Bac Thai, Son La and Lai Chau, where they were expected to eke out a living with what, too often, was a minimum of necessities (see United Nations Fund for Population Activities 1981). The aim was to "move numbers equivalent to the estimated natural increase of the population" (Jones & Fraser 1982, p. 120). There were obvious difficulties in devising and implementing such massive schemes, created partly by poor planning and partly by various natural calamities but, on the whole, the schemes seem to have been a relative success. These resettlement schemes obviously had an effect on the urban population (although without information on the origins of those moved these effects are difficult to quantify). However, they were not aimed specifically at the urban population (as later movements would be).

The actual effects of the industrial–urban policy and these four factors on the urban system are documented in Tables 6.1 and 6.4. First, there was considerable migration into the cities which accounted for the bulk of the total growth of the cities each year (Table 6.4a & b). Most of this migration was apparently the result of "expanding employment in the expanding branches of industry" (Nguyen Thy 1974, p. 353). Secondly, the number of urban places increased, but most of the growth in this expanded urban system was amongst the largest cities, especially Hanoi (note the increase in the two-city primacy index in Table 6.1). Middle-sized cities tended to grow more slowly, and the smaller towns grew little if at all (see Table 6.4c, d, e & f, but note that the effects of "size class jumping" in these tables are likely to be considerable: as they grow in size, certain towns and cities will move up to another size class).

Table 6.4 The Democratic Republic of Vietnam urban system, 1945–70.

(a) Magnitude of rural–urban migration

Period	No. of years	Total	Annual average	% migratory component in total urban population at end of period
1945–55	10	400 000	40 000	40.0
1955–65	10	800 000	80 000	41.2
1965–70	5	−20 000	−4 000	−2.0
1945–70	25	1 180 000	48 000	63.7

(b) Average annual growth of urban population

1945–55	50 000
1955–65	100 000
1965–70	2 000

(c) Distribution of urban places by size classes

Size class	Number of urban places			Share in total number of places %		
	1945	1960	1970	1945	1960	1970
<3000	6	54	46	40.0	58.1	45
3000–20 000	3	27	39	20.0	29.0	39
20 000–50 000	3	9	11	20.0	9.6	11
50 000–100 000	2	1	2	13.0	1.1	2
100 000–200 000	1	1	1	7.0	1.1	1
>200 000	0	1	2	0	1.1	2
total	15	93	101	100	100	100

(d) Changes in total population of size classes of urban places

Size class	Share in total population (%)			Increment (%)
	1945	1960	1970	1945–70
<3000	2.3	10.8	3.8	+1.5
3000–20 000	10.0	12.6	18.2	+8.2
20 000–50 000	16.3	17.3	19.7	−13.4
50 000–100 000	30.6	4.6	5.9	−24.7
100 000–200 000	40.8	12.1	5.4	−34.4
>200 000	0	42.6	47.0	+47.0
total	100.0	100.0	100.0	

(e) Mean size of city by size classes

Size class	1945	1960	1970
<20 000	16 000	4260	5050
20 000–50 000	27 000	28 000	33 000
50 000–100 000	75 000	70 000	54 000
>100 000	200 000	275 000	320 000

Table 6.4—*cont.*

(f) Distribution of cities by growth rates 1960–70

Size class		Number of urban places		
	total	no growth	low rate (mean annual rate <3%)	high rate (mean annual rate >3%)
<3000	46	33	13	0
3000–20 000	39	10	29	0
20 000–50 000	11	0	7	4
50 000–100 000	2	0	0	2
100 000–200 000	1	0	0	1
>200 000	2	0	0	2
total	101	43	49	9

Source: Nguyen Thy (1974).

Zero-urban growth, 1965–73

The wartime period from 1965 to 1973 was a period of zero urban growth. Indeed, the urban population actually declined, in both absolute and relative terms, until about 1973 when bombing of the North was halted. The effects of the war on the urban population were both direct (through actual destruction of urban areas) and indirect (through displacement of population and industry). The direct effects began with the bombing from 1965 to 1968 during which there was widespread destruction in some urban areas, although it was in the period of renewed bombing of the North during 1972–3 that most of the damage was done. The two major cities, Hanoi[3] and Haiphong, were both bombed. All six of the main industrial centres of the North were demolished. Twenty-eight out of 30 provincial capitals were bombed and 12 of them were razed to the ground. Ninety-six out of 116 district capitals were bombed and 12 of them were razed to the ground. About 2700 of the North's 4000 rural villages were bombed and 300 of these were razed (Socialist Republic of Vietnam 1980, Nyland 1981, Westing 1983).

The indirect effects of the bombing were correspondingly great. Over 500 000 people were "evacuated from major cities and minor urban concentrations" (Jones & Fraser 1982, p. 11). In a parallel movement industry was decentralized. Factories were split up and transferred to communes in what was a *de facto* "Maoist" strategy of "industrialization of the countryside", the process underlying any period of zero urban growth.

Re-adjustment and slow urban growth, 1973 to 1975–6

The period from 1973 to 1975–6 was a period of rapid re-adjustment in the North Vietnamese urban system. By 1974, the numbers in the urban population had already reached above the 1965 pre-war level as people streamed back into the cities and the Democratic Republic gradually slipped back into a régime of slow urban growth. However, some of the effects of the war were longer lasting. For example, the population movements to the New Economic Zones, some of which were in response to the exigencies of war (and therefore consisted of some people who originated from urban areas) were made permanent. Thus:

> 11,000 of Thai Binh's inhabitants had gone to the mountain regions to build new economic areas, and tens of thousands of others had joined the army or gone to work on construction sites . . . only 10 per cent failed to overcome the difficulties and had to return to the native villages (*Vietnam Courier* 1974b, p. 14).

Notes

1 This interpretation is at odds with that given by Murray and Szelenyi (1984) who cite North Vietnam as an example of *zero urban growth*, although their figures do not back this interpretation. However, most of the "Maoist" policy of rural industrialization followed by the Democratic Republic was forced on it by circumstances, either war or lack of resources, rather than conscious policy.

2 However, sources we have spoken to suggest that these controls were generally ineffective.

3 Although, generally, only the outskirts of Hanoi were bombed: the central area, with its fine colonial architecture, remains surprisingly unscarred.

7 The Socialist Republic of Vietnam, 1976–85: rebuilding a determinant state

Some months after the fall of Saigon in April 1975 the decision was taken to move to the unification of North and South Vietnam more rapidly. In the autumn, a joint meeting of the Northern leaders and the leaders of the Provisional Revolutionary Government in the South reached agreement on how this political and administrative unification would be organized. Elections were held through the whole of Vietnam for a joint National Assembly in April 1976 and in July the Socialist Republic of Vietnam was established. The Southern Communist Party was integrated into what was now a nationwide Communist Party at the Fourth Congress in December 1976. The NLF was dissolved and its local organizations were absorbed into a National Fatherland Front (Duiker 1983).

The northern state apparatus was now faced with the fairly formidable task of integrating the Northern population of 24½ million with a Southern population of 22 million. Further, this Southern population formed a relatively highly urbanized society with an economy, a state and a civil society with histories and traditions very different from those in the North (Table 7.1). What made the task even more forbidding was that both North and South had been ravaged by warfare. By itself, and given the contradictions of the North Vietnamese state outlined in Chapter 6 and the vagaries of the Vietnamese climate (which proceeded to produce in rapid succession a series of droughts and floods), success could not have been expected overnight. However, the history of the external relations of the new Socialist Republic since 1976 has made the task almost entirely problematic. Indeed, the effect of the incorporation of the South on North Vietnam was sufficiently traumatic that it is possible to wonder whether, as South Vietnamese society went through its

Table 7.1 State, economy and civil society in the pre-1975 Republic of Vietnam.

Sphere	
economy	colonial capitalist/service economy dependent upon USA; agricultural output hit by war
state	dependent upon army
civil society	very heterogeneous; Catholics, Buddhists, Hoa-Hao, Cao-Dai, etc.; Confucian traditions
class composition	small group of indigenous capitalists; large petty bourgeoisie peasantry
external relations	dependent upon USA

"revolutionary" stage, North Vietnamese society did not revert for some time to a "revolutionary" stage as well.

Ideology and external relations in crisis

There have been some shifts in the underlying basis of Vietnamese Communist Party ideology in the period from 1976. At first, the same brand of Marxist–Leninism was followed as before (Ch. 5): in other words, one tempered by nationalism but still quite orthodox:

> Hanoi had even prepared for its victory in the south, in 1975, by reprinting the Vietnamese translation of Lenin's April 1918 treatise on the immediate tasks of the Soviet government; a text in which Lenin specifically recommended the use of mass organisations such as consumers' cooperatives, as a formula for helping revolutionaries to get better control of the distribution of goods. Mekong Delta peasants, after 1975, were thus invited to buy their chickens according to procedures which Lenin had improvised six decades earlier (Woodside 1979, p. 395).

There was the same commitment, amongst the party ideologues, to heavy industry and to the suppression of the petty bourgeoisie.

However, gradually the party line has shifted, partly as a result of the attempts at incorporation of the Southern economy (see below) and partly because of external relations, most especially the move into the Soviet bloc and the war with China. Ideology has had to become more flexible. Socialism has had to be postponed.

The move into the Soviet camp, signified by the continuing ascendancy of Le Duan, continued apace over the whole period of the Second Indochina War, helped by such events as the holding up of Soviet arms shipments sent by rail through China by Beijing and the final withdrawal of all Chinese aid in 1978. The move towards the Soviet bloc was only underlined by the defection to China of a former leading member of the Politburo, Hoang Van Hoan, in the summer of 1979.[1] Thus, in October 1975 major aid agreements were entered into with the USSR, partly as a result of the withdrawal of Chinese aid. In May 1977, Vietnam joined the CMEA financial agencies, the International Bank for Economic Co-operation (IBEC, the CMEA's IMF) and the International Investment Bank (IIB, the CMEA's World Bank). In June 1978 Vietnam joined the CMEA. In November 1978 a 25-year friendship treaty was also signed with the USSR. In 1981 a further four trade agreements were signed involving 40 new major Soviet economic projects and some 100 already in progress (Pike 1982). The list goes on. This is not to say that the relationship with the USSR is perfect. (Soviet moves towards China and the level of Soviet aid have both been criticized in the past.) Nevertheless, it is difficult to see the real alternatives for the Socialist Republic, especially given the pressure exerted by the United States and China to isolate Vietnam both economically and politically.

Vietnam had been at loggerheads with Cambodia since 1975, had been involved in border clashes and even, in October 1977, launched a major thrust into Cambodia. Finally, on December 25, 1978, 13 divisions of the PAVN raced across Cambodia's plains to take over most of that country. It soon became apparent that however deep-rooted in history might be the reasons for the Khmer–Vietnam conflict, "the principal cause behind its escalation was the wider Sino-Vietnamese struggle for influence in the region" (*Far Eastern Economic Review* 1979, p. 319), a judgement only borne out by the Third Indochina War (see Elliott 1980) in which China invaded Vietnam's northern provinces for 17 days in February 1979. The invasion was fought off but Vietnam was, for a time, conducting a

war on two fronts and, in effect, the two wars have continued ever
since – numerous Vietnamese troops are tied up in the Northern
border provinces in case of another Chinese invasion, in Cambodia
(150 000–170 000 troops), principally fending off the Khmer Rouge,
and in Laos (another 60 000 troops).

This situation has been disastrous for Vietnam's *internal* development policies and forms a crucial backdrop to the situation since
1975. The Socialist Republic has to sustain a regular standing army
of a million men and women, and some 40% of the country's annual
budget is regularly devoted to defence. Clearly such a high level of
defence commitment, in a country already racked by shortages
and scarcities, means that valuable resources – ranging from skilled
manpower to money – that could otherwise have been used in
promoting economic development, have had to be diverted from
almost every sector of the economy.

The state in crisis

Throughout the period from 1975 up until the present, the already
war-torn Vietnamese state has been threatened externally by China
and internally by the three contradictions (outlined in Ch. 5) it had
already met in attempting to direct the economy – between a
centrally planned economy and the level of resources needed to plan
the economy, between centralized planning and the need for a
market, and between centralized planning and a practical
requirement for some form of decentralized decision-making. To
these three contradictions there now had to be added what was
effectively a fourth contradiction: that between the societies of
North and South Vietnam. South Vietnam, with its extensive
industry and rich agricultural lands, was a prize of some consequence
but it was also a threat with its large, urban middle class and a host of
other potentially hostile elements. The cumulative result of all these
stresses and strains was a severe crisis of authority for the Vietnamese
state. The task was to rebuild and re-assert this authority.

The contradiction between the capacity of a state-run, centrally
planned economy to control every aspect of society and the level of
resources open to a developing country was highlighted in numerous
ways including the manpower shortages brought about by the wars
of 1978–9 (and the subsequent need to keep up such a large standing

army), frequent paper shortages and the general lack of able administrators.

The contradiction between a centrally planned economy and the
market was continually underlined by the need to rapidly increase
productivity and yet still retain state control of the economy. It was
noticeable that the state-managed sector of the economy (the state
farms, the forestry programmes, the basic construction branches),
the one with the greatest bureaucratic component, was also the sector
where the results of investment and the rate of accumulation of capital
most seriously declined after 1975 (Woodside 1979). This contradiction has not been solved. Rather, in the period since 1975, it has led (as
in many other socialist countries) to a cycle of freeze and thaw in
state–market relations.[2] The situation at present is one of a still:

> unresolved tension or stand-off between the political and
> administrative personnel who believe that socialism means
> economic decision-making by state and party officials and
> whose *raison d'être* has been their role in the planned economy vs
> those (also in the party and government) who believe that it is
> counterproductive to try to control petty commodity produc-
> tion at Vietnam's present level of development (White 1982a,
> p. 24).

The contradiction between centralized planning and decentralized decision-making has similarly resisted solution. This observa-
tion can be tested by considering the history of the *district*, previously
mentioned in Chapter 5. In 1977/8 the Central Committee resolved
that a previously existing local economic and political unit, the
district, should be given greater importance. The resolution stated
the need:

> to firmly build the district into a real agro-industrial economic
> unit and an area for reorganisation of production, organisation
> and redivision of labour, combining industry with agriculture,
> combining the national economy with collective economy, and
> workers with peasants (Central Committee 1977, p. 234).

The country was divided into about 400 districts which would form
"the nucleus of a socialist economy" (*Far Eastern Economic Review*
1978, p. 333), based upon agro-industrial complexes. However, at
first, the plan "met with limited success, as it would necessitate
surrender of power by well-established provincial and cooperative

(village) political and economic institutions" (White 1982a, p. 17). Nevertheless, the reform has now been pressed through (see Central Committee 1982, *Vietnam Courier* 1984) and there are currently 426 districts (*Indochina Chronology* 1985, 4(2), p. 6).

The tensions engendered by each of these three contradictions were, in each case, seriously aggravated by the incorporation of South Vietnam with its much larger scale, and accordingly more complex, economy. Thus, the administrative capacity of the state was stretched to the limit: administrative resources had to be devoted to the South at a time when there were not enough of these resources in the North (and, most especially, they had to be directed to Ho Chi Minh City where many of that city's 500 000 civil servants were in detention, had fled, or did not have the trust of the régime). Then again, the power of the market became a more serious threat: market relations were engrained in the South and in much of Southern society (especially amongst the urban middle class and the peasants of the Mekong Delta). Such elements proved resistant to socialization of the economy. Yet the state could not afford to push socialization of the vital Southern agricultural sector too far if it was to keep productivity high in a time of serious food shortages. Finally, after the war, decentralization was a fact in the rural areas of the South; the problem for the state was how to centralize.

However, what made the South an even worse problem, one which meant that it could almost be elevated to the status of a contradiction in itself, was the *reciprocal effect* that the incorporation of the South had upon the various Northern state apparatuses. This effect can be shown by the example of the Vietnamese Communist Party (Table 7.2) (see Turley 1980a, Elliott 1981, Thayer 1982). The party grew at a rate of 70 000–80 000 members per annum through the late 1970s and early 1980s. However, in 1983 its growth had slowed considerably, to only 36 000 in the year. Still, the party's growth has been considerable since unification. But, in the South the party apparatus has remained weak. For example, as late as 1982, party membership in Ho Chi Minh City was only 40 000 and many of these members had been drafted in from the North. There was tension between these Northern cadres and the Southerners. However, worse than this, the North Vietnamese cadres began to follow a pattern of Southern needs and wants, especially for consumer goods. Corruption and theft seem, from recent reports, to be on the increase, even in the security forces in the North (*Far Eastern*

Table 7.2 The membership of the Vietnamese Communist Party.

Year	Total	North Vietnam	South Vietnam
1945	5000		
1946	20 000		
1947	50 000		
1948	168 000	102 000	23 000
1950	700 000		
1955			15 000
1959			5 000
1960		500 000	
1962			35 000
1966			100 000
1968		800 000	
1970	1 300 000	1 100 000	200 000
1976	1 553 500		
1978			273 000
1982	1 928 300		
1983	1 964 300		

Source: Elliott (1981), *Far Eastern Economic Review* (1984).

Economic Review 1981, Hastings 1982, Quinn-Judge 1982). In 1980 a campaign was begun to weed out the anti-social elements in the party. Those who committed "serious errors" such as corruption, bribery and oppression did not have their membership cards renewed. One report speaks of 200 000 memberships having been purged (Chanda 1982a) and a parallel recruitment drive was put into effect.

In summary then, the apparatuses of the Socialist Republic state throughout the period from 1975 to at least 1981 were in some disarray as they tried to adjust to running a larger and more complex country than previously while also initiating new rounds of national economic planning. It is no surprise, then, that Woodside (1979) writes of the "bureaucratic incoherence" of the Socialist Republic state.[3]

The economy in crisis

In May 1975 the economy of the whole of Vietnam was in crisis. In the North, the effects of the Second Indochina War lingered on two years after the cessation of the bombing. The Southern economy was in chaos, yet, if the loss of billions of dollars of US aid could be overcome it clearly had great potential in view of the industry of Saigon (now renamed Ho Chi Minh City) and the vast rice bowl of the Mekong Delta.[4]

Industrial policy took two related forms. First, Southern industry and markets had to be socialized. However, the new Provisional Revolutionary Government of the South was cautious. *Hoc Tap*, the Party's theoretical journal, argued for a soft line. Thus, in April 1975, readers were told:

> . . . as an immediate goal, it is necessary to guide, encourage and help the private economic sector, so that it will devote its capabilities to developing production and business activities to the benefit of national welfare and the people's livelihood (quoted in Nyland 1981, p. 438).

This approach was pragmatically defended by the Chairman of the Provisional Revolutionary Government in the South "on the grounds that the new administration simply did not have either the resources or the organisation to do otherwise" (Nyland 1981, p. 439)

However, in September 1975, nothing daunted, the Provisional Revolutionary Government began to take steps to socialize the industry and markets of the South. A 14-point economic programme was introduced and the currency was changed. In October 1975 the *comprador* bourgeoisie – mainly ethnic Chinese from the Cholon area of Saigon – were rounded up. This group constituted a major threat to the new régime, since through their buying power they were able to manipulate market prices and compete with the state to purchase foodstuffs.

> Their influence on all levels of the (Southern) economy was enormous. According to one survey: the Chinese in Vietnam monopolised not only the rice trade but the associated processing, distribution and credit sectors as well. In 1974, the Chinese community reportedly controlled 50 per cent of all retail trade; 80 per cent of the food, textile, chemical, metallurgical, engineering and electrical industries; 70 per cent of the import/export trade and nearly 100 per cent of the wholesale trade. Other indicators speak of Chinese commercial prowess: ownership of 42 of 60 major companies, receipt of 80 per cent of

all bank loans and responsibility for two thirds of all annual investment in Southern Vietnam (Thayer 1982, p. 16).

The new Five Year Plan (1975–80) had to be rapidly reformulated to include the South. This second Five Year Plan was fairly conventional and was based upon the need to develop both agriculture (30% of investment funds) and industry (35% of investment funds).

In the North industry was to be rebuilt. In the South there was to be a gradual transition from privately owned to state-owned industry. "While the government would make use of the scientific and technical cadres of the old regime, it would transform private industry . . . through joint state–private enterprise . . ." (*Far Eastern Economic Review* 1978, p. 329). In line with the directives of the plan, the larger Southern manufacturing enterprises were gradually transformed into joint state–private enterprises and thence to state enterprises. Thus:

> 1,500 large and small scale capitalist enterprises were nationalized and reconverted into 650 national enterprises with 130,000 workers or 70 per cent of the total of those working in private capitalist enterprises. The mixed national – private industrial enterprises (state–private capital) assumed (*sic*) 70 per cent of industrial production (Nguyen Khac Vien cited in Thayer 1982, p. 29).

By early 1978, the state had also taken over control of the transport and construction sectors as well as many handicraft, marketing and consumer operations (Table 7.3). However, a substantial proportion of the Southern economy still remained outside state control and in private hands. In particular, the majority of smaller trading enterprises, forming as much as 65% of the South's retail market, remained in private hands until March 1978. Indeed, Turley (1980b, p. 48) reports that the number of small private Southern traders actually increased from 1975 to 1978. However, the facts of ownership concealed a far more serious situation, for not only were the petty bourgeoisie competing with the state trade sector in the purchase of commodities (see Duiker 1980, Thayer 1982) but:

> After 1975, the overseas Chinese businessmen in Ho Chi Minh City continued to ally themselves with private, resilient, "centipede-legged" trading networks in the Mekong Delta which were based upon the central personages (as some cadres

Table 7.3 Industrial employment in the Socialist Republic of Vietnam, 1976–9 (thousands).

	1976	1977	1978	1979
(a) State sector				
energy, fuel	49.3	53.1	50.7	51.4
iron and steel	27.2	29.3	31.1	28.9
engineering	90.4	105.9	113.7	123.9
chemicals	39.6	43.8	48.2	54.9
construction materials, cellulose, paper	132.0	197.7	151.8	163.8
food processing	63.5	67.8	73.4	74.3
textiles, clothing, leather	96.7	104.2	105.6	108.9
printing, books	11.1	12.7	13.1	14.5
other	10.4	11.9	7.3	7.1
total	519.2	576.4	549.9	627.7
(b) Artisans and industrial co-operatives				
energy, fuel	1.7	1.4	1.3	1.4
engineering	106.1	134.3	151.5	161.8
chemicals	24.3	22.3	24.2	26.4
construction materials, cellulose, paper	520.9	535.6	543.1	551.3
food processing	549.2	554.4	514.1	495.3
textiles, clothing, leather	248.5	276.1	296.7	309.4
printing, books	43.0	44.0	39.4	41.0
other	20.5	21.1	20.1	23.5
total	1514.2	1589.2	1590.4	1610.1

Source: Nguyen Duc Nhuan (1984b), p. 330.

belatedly discovered) of southern villages, namely entrepreneurially minded 'middle-peasants' who could astutely calculate marketing and transportation costs. In the south's cities, such businessmen preserved their firms by signing economic management contracts with the state which allowed them to continue to own production materials. Or if the firms were 'reconstructed' into state enterprises or mixed public–private enterprises, they were allowed to dominate the directorial committees which exercised authority over the new businesses, usually outnumbering the worker members on such committees by ratios of as high as ten to one. Party cadres in the

south were 'flattered' by the overseas Chinese 'capitalists' so
effectively that many of them 'lost their class viewpoint', aban-
doning interest in the cultivation of mass labour unions, and
even conniving with the capitalists to steal state property
(Woodside 1979, p. 402).

This then, was a direct challenge to the Socialist Republic state by the
Southern petty bourgeoisie which could not go unanswered.

In February 1978, Nguyen Van Linh, a member of the Political
Bureau and the Chairman of the Committee for the Transformation
of Private Industry and Trade in the South, was dismissed from that
office (although he remains an important figure as the Secretary of
the Ho Chi Minh City Communist Party and a member of the
Central Committee). He was replaced by his deputy and Political
Bureau alternate, Do Muoi. This dismissal was the prelude to a
full-scale assault on private commerce that began on March 23, 1978
and which was foreshadowed in newspaper editorials, government
reports and at conferences in the previous year (see, for details,
Duiker 1980, Turley 1980b, Thayer 1982). Private trade was transferred to socialist trade organizations, and many shopkeepers were only
allowed to continue to retail goods "until they could be shifted to
production". Those businesses allowed to remain open had to agree
to sell their products to the state. By the summer of 1978, 30 000
businesses had been closed in the South, many of them owned by
ethnic Chinese; 30 000 southern merchants and 150 000 dependants
were affected. Owners were paid compensation and given the choice
of working as employees of the state or moving to the New Economic Zones. Many of them found another choice: they left the country
to become refugees. Nyland (1981, p. 443) dramatically describes the
dismantling of the Southern petty bourgeoisie:

the party mobilised tens of thousands of youth volunteers,
cadres and the military. All businesses were ordered to remain
closed until after an inventory of their stocks had been made and
guards were placed on these goods to ensure they could not be
dispersed before Government could collect them.

On the 3rd of May, this initial attack . . . was followed by a
second currency reform. This reform, involving the introduction of a single new currency for the whole country . . . was
handled in a much more efficient manner than the reforms of
1975. The Government imposed tight restrictions on how

much a family could retain in cash and made it obligatory for non-businessmen to explain where their money came from if they tried to exchange funds above a 500 Dong ceiling.

The currency reform together with the expropriation of the property of large traders and speculators was successful . . . in bringing greater control of the country's economy under the Government . . . By the end of June the Government was able to announce that 95 per cent of 'bourgeois traders' households in Ho Chi Minh City had registered for productive work and 70 per cent had left for various provinces to help establish new industries or to take part in agriculture. The newspaper *Tin Sang*, however, admitted on 15 April that 'some have preferred to commit suicide rather than adopt a new way of life which they regarded as a form of deportation'. It should also be added that many of those forced to abandon their former trade rather than going to the new economic zones joined the exodus of those leaving the country.

In effect, the state closed down a considerable part of the South Vietnamese economy. Now the contradiction between a centrally planned economy and the market was cruelly exposed. The problem was not just that a part of the industrial and commercial sector was left lying idle by these activities, there was also a problem of the co-ordination of what was left. For example, the closure of nearly every shop in the Cholon area of Ho Chi Minh City meant that the government had to open 4000 state-managed shops and find managers for them, managers who necessarily were not (at least initially) skilled (see *Far Eastern Economic Review* 1979).

There was, as well, a knock-on effect of this series of policy measures in the South. Many Northern ethnic Chinese, interpreting the attacks on the Southern petty bourgeoisie (with some justification) as anti-Chinese, left the country and their departure adversely affected the running of both light and heavy industries in the North, and especially textiles and coal mining.

It is not therefore too much of a surprise to find that after this dramatic freeze there came a thaw. In 1979, the Sixth Plenum of the Fourth Congress of the Vietnamese Communist Party produced a set of "New Economic Policies". In particular, Resolution 6 "affirmed the legality and legitimacy of private individual enterprise in the period of transition to socialism" (Nguyen Khac Vien 1982a, p. 21).

According to the new economic policies, privately organized, small-scale production now again had an important rôle to play, particularly in the production of consumer goods, and especially now that the *comprador* bourgeoisie was officially declared extinct (see Central Committee 1982). "If it is considered that some types of state-produced goods can be better produced and developed by the handicrafts and artisan industry and private capitalists, they must be boldly assigned to the latter" (cited in Thayer 1982, p. 41). Resolution 6 had its critics, however. Le Duc Tho, for example, "argued at some length that any deficiencies in the state and party's management of the economy should be remedied by improving rather than decreasing, administrative control of the economy" (White 1982a, p. 23). Be that as it may, a number of other market-related measures were subsequently introduced into industry, including piece-rate wages and profit–loss accounting systems. The result was that the population of the South (and, to a lesser extent, the North) responded with a proliferation of small businesses.

However, by 1982 it had become apparent that the freedom offered by Resolution 6 had led to something approaching chaos in some parts of the South, and most especially in the trading sector (which in turn, affected the ability of the state to set prices). Free-wheeling firms and various provincial import–export companies had set up their own lines of supply and began to bid against each other; the situation led to considerable inflation and corruption. As one Central Committee member, Hoang Tung, put it, "it became apparent that in an effort to allow more dynamism and initiative at the lower levels while maintaining planning leadership at the centre, we had let free-market priorities get out of hand" (cited in Shaplen 1985a, p. 116). (The situation was exacerbated by the state's policy of offering food subsidies to party workers, pensioners and others, since the rising cost of buying some of this food on the free market (and abroad) became an ever-increasing burden on state expenditure.)

Thus a whole series of clarifying reforms were brought in. Enormous increases were made in taxes on antique shops, restaurants and other "socially undesirable" businesses. Traders were required to deposit capital in state banks. Reminders of who was in control, such as the seizure of the houses of traders who could not explain their wealth, were widely publicized. However, these reforms did not mean that the hard-line ideologues were getting their way. The underlying direction of policy, as revealed by the Sixth Plenum of the Fifth Party Congress held in the summer of 1984, was still towards liberalization. Hoang Tung stated: "It did not change the initiative given to local and provincial establishments, but it clarified and specified areas where policy was being misconstrued and misinterpreted by failure to abide by central guidelines" (cited in Shaplen 1985a, p. 116). The Eighth Plenum of the Vietnamese Communist Party Central Committee has since gone even further:

> The age of economic planning by 'administrative order' is over, the Plenum announced after its 10–17 June (1985) session. Bureaucratic centralism is to be eliminated, it said in a communique and 'financial autonomy' encouraged. All government concerns are to be responsible for their own profits and losses, with all 'subsidies for irrational losses' by government enterprises to end (Quinn-Judge 1985, p. 36).

What, then, has been the net effect of these attempts at socialization of industry in the South (and also in the North)? In 1979, a newspaper article could claim, correctly enough, that:

> By now, the State has taken control of most of the major and medium-sized processing installations (in the South) and abolished the commercial enterprises of big capitalists, chief speculators and heads of granaries . . . (and has been able) to establish initial systems for collecting, purchasing and distributing grain and foodstuffs in various provinces and cities (quoted in Nyland 1981, p. 445).

However, since then, the state has been forced to liberalize controls over small industry – and its control over the market for goods has often become all but non-existent. In all some 70% of goods in circulation are now controlled by the free market. "Socialist" trading represents about 50% of wholesale trade and 45% of retail trade (*Far Eastern Economic Review* 1984). Again, forms of ownership are still quite diverse. Whereas in the North there are only three such forms – state-owned, collective and private – in the South there are five forms of ownership – state-owned, collective, combined privately-owned and state-owned, small capitalist, and industrial entrepreneur (Shaplen 1985b). The situation is that "we now have two parallel markets. One is organized and state directed, with stable prices. The other is the free market which operates according to supply and demand. *Things would be easier if our state were strong enough to control the whole market, but it isn't; our state is not rich enough"* (Nguyen Khac Vien 1982b, p. 379, our emphasis).

The policy now is one of more gradual socialization of industry and the free markets, "we are adopting a gradual approach to socialism. Small traders will slowly turn into producers for the government, while others will be agents for government-owned enterprises, or we will make them that. Small producers can be organized collectively" (Le Quang Chanh, cited in Shaplen 1985b, p. 99). However, considerable concessions to the free market are still being made. For example, in 1985 food subsidies to many state employees were ended.

The second form that was taken by industrial policy, one which of course went hand in hand with the socialization of production, was the expansion of production. It is fair to say that this expansion was not achieved. The targets set by the second Five Year Plan (1975–80) were extremely ambitious given Vietnam's straitened circumstances. By 1980, only two-thirds of the targets that were set in 1975 had been reached (Thayer 1982). In fact, some targets were missed spectacularly, helped by a combination of the Chinese invasion of the Northern provinces which in particular destroyed a power station and the apatite mine that was the country's main source of fertilizer, and disastrous droughts and floods. In 1978, for example:

> Gross industrial output was expected to increase by 21.7 per cent over 1977. In a half-yearly assessment *Nhan Dan* noted that 'industrial production has fallen short of the set quotas, recording an increase of nearly 7 per cent only' over 1977. The paper sharply criticised bad leadership, despotic bureaucracy and a lack of a sense of responsibility, and said that as a result 'machinery and equipment had been only half utilised and worked for an average of only four or five hours a day'. Another article earlier in the year said that workers only put in an average of 22 days a month, leading to very low productivity (*Far Eastern Economic Review* 1979, p. 322).

While, in 1979, the invasion made matters even worse:

> Industry, which has been suffering from the lack of raw materials and spare parts, was further affected by the Chinese aid cut and the diversion of limited foreign exchange to import grain.

A number of factories had to be closed completely for lack of raw materials. Drops in coal production – due, in part to the departure of ethnic Chinese miners – also affected power generation and, in consequence, the industrial output.

Since the industrial output in 1978 grew by 7 per cent compared with the target of 21 per cent, the 1979 target was realistically lowered to a 12 per cent increase. But it was highly doubtful whether even this could be achieved. The mining sector, which represents 5 per cent of GNP, was seriously affected by the Chinese invasion. Iron ore and phosphate mines in Lao Cai, and tin, copper and chromium mines in the Long San and Lao Bang areas were damaged. The French-built aniseed-oil factory near Long San was also destroyed.

The poor economic performance of the Socialist Republic until 1980 can be seen from Table 7.4.

In the light of these past failures the main thrust of the third Five Year Plan (1982–6) was oriented towards agriculture and light industry, and especially the production of consumer goods (Chanda 1981a,b)[5] and away from heavy industry. "Unlike the grandiose past plan, which fell apart, the new plan emphasises small, practical projects, with steady growth matched to human needs" (Morrow 1982, p. 49). A primary aim was:

to coordinate the development of industry and agriculture. We're not talking simply about the coordination of a few big, heavy industries. If you go down to the local level, to a district, to a cooperative, right there the people will have industrial units.

Table 7.4   Index of productive national income of the Socialist Republic of Vietnam, 1976–80, 1975 = 100.

	1976	1977	1978	1979	1980
total	114.6	116.9	119.6	119.1	113.4
industry	119.5	139.3	143.1	137.1	126.6
construction	126.0	133.5	151.3	129.9	100.6
agriculture and forestry	104.8	100.1	100.5	104.9	106.9
trade and material supply	139.4	137.3	145.7	144.8	128.5

Source: Socialist Republic of Vietnam (1981).

Another aim seemed to be to replicate the Northern economy in the South.

> In the North every district has a machine shop. This machine shop will make small machines for agriculture, hand tools and carts; it will make all the basic necessities for agriculture in that district (Le Hong Tam 1980, p. 24).

The new Five Year Plan, together with the relaxation of the state's hold on the market and, latterly, a contract system of production, divergences in wage scales for different grades of workers and wages tied to productivity, seems to have contributed to a marked improvement in Vietnam's overall economic performance after the toughest years of 1978 and 1979. For example, since 1980 Vietnam's GNP has increased at an average of 7.8% per annum. Industrial production increased at an average of 11.9% per annum over the same period, with as much as a 15% increase in 1984 (Shaplen 1985a, p. 122). However, the state of industry remains generally poor, running at 50% of capacity as a result of shortages of raw materials, electric power[6] and spare parts. Some of the shortages interrelate: Vietnam has large reserves of coal, iron ore and bauxite but since these are still produced in relatively small quantities, there is little hope of any sizeable aluminium or steel industry. These kinds of log-jams will not be solved quickly or easily.

Once again, agricultural developments are already well covered in the literature (e.g. Nyland 1981; Thayer 1982; White 1982a,b, 1983; Appleton 1983) and only the briefest of summaries will be given here. A series of successive natural calamities including floods, drought and typhoons in the period from 1976 to 1980[7] combined with widespread and enduring war damage[8] and over zealous attempts to force the collectivization of agriculture in the South to produce general food shortages. Food was therefore the major concern of the new Socialist Republic, effectively overriding industrial development since most available foreign exchange had to go on buying in grain, rice and fertilizer (Vietnam still has to import 1 million tonnes of fertilizer a year as a result of the Chinese destruction of the Lao Cai mine). Indeed, the events of 1978 were as much stimulated by the need to move against capitalist trade in rice as by any industrial considerations. In 1978 and 1979 the food situation became critical (see Tables 5.1, 7.5 & 7.6), especially in the North. Food production:

Table 7.5 The Socialist Republic of Vietnam agricultural sector: total value of agricultural production, 1976–80 (at constant 1975 prices).

	1976	1977	1978	1979	1980
Value (million dong)	7087.8	6740.2	6743.6	7204.1	7662.5
agriculture	5663.4	5205.4	5410.8	5767.3	6211.5
food crops	4064.8	3731.5	3731.5	4154.0	4401.5
livestock and poultry	1424.4	1534.8	1332.8	1436.8	1411.0
livestock	577.8	524.7	478.4	577.9	570.2
Index (%, 1975 = 100)					
total	110.2	104.8	104.9	112.0	118.6
agriculture	112.9	103.8	107.9	115.0	123.9
food crops	117.5	108.0	107.9	120.1	127.3
livestock and poultry	100.7	108.5	94.2	101.5	99.7
livestock	105.1	95.4	87.0	105.1	103.7
Structure %					
total	100.0	100.0	100.0	100.0	100.0
agriculture	79.9	77.2	80.2	80.0	81.5
food crops	57.3	55.4	55.3	57.7	57.7
livestock and poultry	20.1	22.8	19.8	20.0	18.5
livestock	8.1	7.8	7.1	8.0	7.5

Source: Socialist Republic of Vietnam (1981).

reached a record natural low of twelve million nine hundred thousand tons (in 1978). This meant that the average Vietnamese received only two hundred and fifty-one kilograms of food last year. In contrast, between 1965 and 1973 the northerners themselves grew enough to supply each of their citizens with three hundred and twelve kilograms, and since the Chinese were donating about half a million tons of rice annually, the actual per capita figure was three hundred and twenty-four kilograms (Shaplen 1985a, p. 114)

In the autumn of 1980 there were food riots in Haiphong and in Nghe Tinh province, and open expressions of discontent amongst the citizens of Hanoi (Chanda 1981b). These protests from the heartland of the state could not go unheard. Resolution 6 was aimed at agriculture as much if not more than at industry and the debates of the time contain some remarkable self-criticism. For example, an

October 1979 editorial in the newspaper *Nhan Dan*, entitled "Plan and Market", boldly pronounced:

The simple mentality of wanting all production and distribution to be taken in hand by administrative laws and regulations immediately, and eliminating everything else by not allowing anyone to do anything outside of nationalised industries and cooperatives and forbidding all forms of uncontrolled exchange can only lead to an economic situation of poverty and low growth (quoted in White 1982a, p. 23).

A number of initiatives have been introduced into the countryside in response to this new policy of liberalization. These have included encouraging co-operatives to subcontract their land to co-operative households for cultivation for all but the initial steps (White 1982a), allowing land not used by co-operatives to become available to individuals willing to cultivate it, enabling virgin land brought into production to be free from tax for five years, and permitting all produce above a compulsory minimum that has to be sold to the state to be sold on the free market (Nyland 1981). These liberalizing policies should be seen, however, against the background of the gradual collectivization of the South, which began in 1977–8.

By May, 1980, 1,747 cooperatives, 16,801 agricultural production collectives and 303 collectives specialising in operating agricultural machinery had been established. Despite this impressive expansion these organisations have only been able to induce the participation of 50 per cent of peasant families and are using only 36 per cent of the total cultivated land (Nyland 1981, p. 44).

In fact, the policy of collectivization has been successful in the poorer areas of the South and especially in parts of Central Vietnam, where conditions were ripe. By 1983, Central Vietnam was declared collectivized (although often this was in appearance only) (*Far Eastern Economic Review* 1984). In the Mekong Delta, which the state saw as the nation's granary, collectivization has been more patchy, even though taxes are lower for those who join collectives. This is not surprising in an area where peasants were already relatively well-off and displayed a number of individualist cultural traits. It is clearly still against the economic interests of a number of the Mekong peasants to join co-operatives and will remain so as long as some basic agricultural commodities (like pork, poultry and fruit) still escape government control to a great extent (Quinn-Judge 1985). Be this as it may, by 1985, 75% of the cultivated areas of South Vietnam were nominally in the hands of collectives and co-operatives (*Indochina Chronology* 1985, 4(2), p. 8).

Certainly, however, the measures announced in Resolution 6 combined with the added acreage brought back into production[9] and technical improvements such as improved irrigation and the use of new strains of short-term growth, high-yield rice seem to have helped considerably (Table 7.6). In 1983, the Socialist Republic apparently became self-sufficient in food for the first time, with an increase in the "food share" per person from 268 kg in 1980 to 300 kg. However, this still means that even raw agricultural production is only barely keeping pace with population growth. There is no surplus to allow for more livestock breeding or the accumulation of a reserve. In particular, although post-war yields have increased over pre-war yields in the North, in the South they remain near stationary (Westing 1983). Until this problem of low Southern yields is solved, Vietnamese agriculture will remain in a state of near-crisis.

Table 7.6 The Socialist Republic of Vietnam agricultural sector: crop production, 1975–85.

	1975	1979	1980	1981	1982	1983	1984	1985
production (million tons)	11.4	13.9	14.1	15.5	16.6	17.0	18.0★	19.0–20.0★

★Estimate. Note the comparable table in Nguyen Duc Nhuan (1984b, p. 328).
Source: *Indochina Chronology* (1983, 2(4), p. 11.

Civil society in crisis

Vietnamese civil society took on a markedly different character as soon as the South was incorporated. At unification 2 million Catholics were added to the 1–1.2 million in the North, and a further 1.2–1.5 million ethnic Chinese were added to the 300 000 Northern ethnic Chinese. Then again, the South also included within its borders a very large Buddhist element (nominally 90% of the population), as well as about 2 million followers of the modified Buddhist sect, the Hoa-Hao, and about 500 000 members of the syncretic Cao-Dai sect. Further, there was a strong Confucian tradition. Amongst all these different cultural groups were many that had a long history of hostility to communism. Indeed, many members of these groups had fled from the North in the previous two decades to escape the Northern régime.

The South, then, had a civil society very different from that of the North. This was not only because one society lived under a socialist régime and the other a capitalist. It was also a function of more subtle cultural minutiae. For example, in 1967 Fall (p. 185) could already note that, in the North:

> a whole new technical vocabulary is being created, borrowing chiefly from the Chinese, but from the Russians as well. In many cases, the North Vietnamese neologisms have nothing in common with synonymous terms being coined in the south. Thus the division of Viet-Nam into two states is being deepened far beyond the difference of political and social systems.

To cope with these divisions, the new Socialist Republic devised a number of strategies. With some of the less threatening elements, it came to an uneasy accommodation. For example, the state struck up a truce of sorts with Southern Catholics and Buddhists, which in the case of the Catholics allowed the religion to keep operating, but placed restrictions upon the number of priests and their replacement. Many Buddhist nuns and priests were persuaded to leave the movement, and Buddhist schools and orphanages were taken over; however, Buddhism continues (Shaplen 1985b). With other elements, outright repression seems to have been the order of the day. The Cao-Dai and Hoa-Hao, both of which had been actively anti-communist, have been badly treated, and the ethnic Chinese (who originally had a special status), given their always questionable loyalty, worsening external relations with China and largely middle-class membership, left in droves from both North and South after 1978. In this general climate of fear and uncertainty the state seemed unsure what to do with other potentially resistant elements and, as a result, probably simply aggravated the situation. The ethnic minorities of the Northern border provinces are a case in point. Although previously well treated in the North (indeed, they formed an essential part of the revolution), they now found their loyalty in doubt under the barrage of Chinese propaganda. The Autonomous Zones were divided in 1976 and a number of ethnic leaders were removed from responsible state positions (although others were added). In the South, the hostility of many of the ethnic minorities of the Central Highlands was only fuelled by attempts to make them engage in settled cultivation and by the settling of ethnic Vietnamese in their areas from the Plains Provinces. There is, for example, at least one insurgent group that may still be operating in the Central Highlands – FULRO (Front Uni pour La Lutte des Races) – apart from the more shadowy Front for the Salvation of Vietnam and similarly named groups.

The more general strategy of the state to control Southern civil society concentrated upon all the paraphernalia of socialist socialization previously used in the North (Ch. 5). However, once again, education has been the primary tool of socialization. For example, in the South the schools were nationalized and all the textbooks they had formerly used were banned:

> textbooks on social sciences and history were rewritten and courses in Marxism–Leninism were introduced. Under the new system emphasis was placed on linking study with work and schools were set up in working-class districts, mountain areas and new economic zones. The Government also claimed that almost a million southerners (65 per cent of the total number of illiterate people) 'were freed from illiteracy' (*Far Eastern Economic Review* 1978, p. 330).

However, once again, the contradiction between the state's expansion into Southern civil society and its resources has been a crucial one. Many schools are part-time: even in Hanoi schools work on four-hour shifts (*Far Eastern Economic Review* 1980).

Notes

1   Hoang Van Hoan's (admittedly biased) but hardly novel analysis of Vietnam was this:

> Vietnam today is no longer an independent and sovereign country but one subservient to a foreign power economically, politically, militarily and diplomatically. If this state of affairs should be allowed to continue, it would not be long before Vietnam turns into

a source of raw materials, a processing plant and a military base serving the interests of a foreign power (cited in Honey 1979, p. 4).

2   One which seems likely to continue into the foreseeable future.
3   Thus, not only were there the normal problems of co-ordination between ministries in developing the same plan common to all centrally planned economies but the Vietnamese state also often lacked even the rules to govern the form and content of this co-ordination. For example:

> Rather than citing a scarcity of foreign aid, or the unmodern mentalities of Vietnamese peasants, as the chief obstruction to the introduction of advanced technology into Vietnamese farming the Under-secretary of the Ministry of Agriculture, Duong Hong Dat, explained in an interview in the summer of 1978 that the major difficulty was the Vietnamese state's institutional immaturity. Vietnam lacked the 'legal bases' for an agriculture revolution, the 'state regulations' or the 'laws' which could govern the work of different economic branches and localities (Woodside 1979, p. 399).

The typical Vietnamese bureaucrat's mandarin ways further stressed the situation. He or she "slowed the government processes by his (or her) situational concern for being both overbearingly solemn and excessively obsequious . . . but his (or her) chief interest was in establishing time-consuming 'favour-granting' psychologies" (Woodside 1979, p. 401).

4   Traditionally, the North has not been agriculturally self-sufficient, whereas the South has always maintained a comfortable surplus.
5   However, the existence of this plan should not be read as ending the commitment to a heavy industry path to development: rather, it is a postponement.
6   A huge hydroelectric scheme at Hoa Binh, south-west of Hanoi, is meant to come on stream in 1987 which will improve the situation. Two other schemes are planned for the South. The problem then will become the reconstruction of the country's electricity grid!
7   These floods, droughts and typhoons have continued into the 1980s. For example, in 1983 the year's output of food was achieved despite a series of typhoons and lesser storms which destroyed as much as 400 000 tonnes of rice crop.
8   War damage was particularly severe in the South (Westing 1983) and had marked effects on silviculture, fisheries and agriculture (Table 5.6). For example, forest damage is estimated at 100 000 ha of forest completely obliterated by cratering (perhaps 1% of the entire South Vietnamese forest), 50 000 ha of forest completely obliterated by chemical agents (or 0.5% of the South Vietnamese forest) and another 1.3 million ha (or 12% of the South Vietnamese forest) partially damaged by chemical agents. Another 325 000 ha of land (or approximately 3% of the South Vietnamese forest) was totally cleared by tractors. Combining these estimates and allowing for multiple damage, complete or essentially complete devastation of South Vietnam's upland forest amounted to 417 000 ha, representing 4% of total forestland. In addition, an estimated

124 000 ha (or 41%) of South Vietnam's mangrove habitat was completely destroyed by chemical agents (Westing 1983).

Agricultural damage in the South as a result of the Second Indochina War included the deaths of 900 000 water buffalo, the destruction of about 40% of rubber plantation trees, and chemical crop destruction, estimated to have affected at least 40 000 ha of agricultural land. Westing (1983) estimates that 400 000 ha of South Vietnam's agricultural land was put out of commission during the war.

9 Agricultural acreage was added by the New Economic Zone programme (see Ch. 9) but this programme has contributed very little to overall agricultural production since so many of these zones are being founded on relatively unsuitable land. However, greater hopes can be laid on the replanting of rubber, coffee and tea plantations which is already having effects on the Vietnamese balance of payments.

8 *Urbanization in the Socialist Republic of Vietnam, 1976–85*

The condition of the Southern cities must have given the North Vietnamese leadership considerable pause when compared to the situation in the North in 1954 (Turley 1977a). First, there was a much larger urban population forming nearly 43% of the total population (on 1971 figures). Such concentrations of population were much more difficult to control than had been the case in the North in 1954. Given the small size of the Provisional Revolutionary Government state apparatus, some degree of accommodation had to be reached. Secondly, there was no orderly transfer of power. As a result, the cities were still filled to overflowing with refugees. Thus Thayer (1982) notes that perhaps as many as 10 million people were displaced in the period from 1965 to 1975, representing about 47% of the total Southern population. Many of those displaced went to the cities. Thirdly, the population was not acquiescent. The Southern cities were inhabited by people who had fled the Northern régime, by large Chinese communities (more than half a million in Saigon alone) and by the massive military establishment of the Republic of Vietnam.

In one respect, however, the Northern cities of 1954 were the ancestors of the Southern cities of 1975, if on a vastly smaller scale. They were each colonial cities, based upon the economy of another country and therefore unable to continue in that rôle when access to the metropolitan economy was denied. However, in the South, service economies like those of Saigon or Cam Ranh had reached a grandiose scale. As Table 8.1 shows, the Republic of Vietnam did not have a balance of payments: rather, it relied upon billions of dollars of US aid.

Imports of consumer goods, encouraged to prevent galloping inflation were financed in large part by the US sponsored

Table 8.1 The Republic of Vietnam balance of payments 1969–73 (in US $ millions).

	1969	1970	1971	1972	1973
exports (free on board)	16.0	12.7	14.7	23.8	56.3
imports (cost, insurance, freight)	853.2	778.8	802.7	742.7	828.6

Source: Nguyen Duc Nhuan (1978).

Commercial Import Program. Several hundred thousand Vietnamese worked for US agencies in South Vietnam or otherwise served the needs of the large foreign population (Duiker 1983, p. 101).

Furthermore the black market had reached epic proportions.

What, then, was the condition of the South Vietnamese cities before unification? This is a subject that is already well covered in the literature (e.g. Ng Shui Meng 1974, Pressat 1974, Nguyen Duc Nhuan 1977, 1978) and we will therefore deal with it only briefly. Figure 6.1 and Tables 8.2 and 8.3 show that the urban population of the South grew very rapidly from 1958 to 1975.[1] Throughout this period Saigon showed a high degree of primacy, but Table 8.3 shows that, relative to the total urban population, the percentage of the population living in the Saigon agglomeration actually decreased during the period before 1975, whereas other cities grew much faster. Da Nang, the second largest Southern city, is typical of what war can do to urban population growth. Thus, in just one year between 1967 and 1968 its population rose by 58 300 or 21.1% as a result of the Tet offensive. After the Easter 1972 offensive its population rose by a further 20 311 or 4.6% over the previous year (Ng Shui Meng 1974). Although much of the movement into the Southern cities from 1958 to 1975 was therefore the result of refugees fleeing from the war, it is important to note that the component of ordinary migrants was also high, which meant that at the end of the war it was by no means certain that there would be any large outflow of people (see Goodman & Franks 1975).

In 1975 the cadres of the North Vietnamese state (and the Provisional Revolutionary Government) were therefore faced with serious problems of "hyperurbanization" in the South and still

Table 8.2 The growth of the population of the 19 largest Republic of Vietnam towns (in thousands)*.

	1955†	1960	1964	1968	1970	1971	1974–5†
Saigon							
agglomeration	1000	2296	2431	3156	3320	3500	4000–4500
town	—	1400	1600	1682	1761	1804	1860
Da Nang	50	104	149	334	385	438	500–600
Quy Nhon	—	31	50	114	170	189	240
Hue	—	103	110	160	184	200	210
Nha Trang	—	49	53	102	106	195	200–400
Can Tho	—	49	60	88	116	154	180
My Tho	—	40	63	80	110	110	120
Cam Ranh	—	—	31	66	76	104	120
Vung Tau	—	—	49	70	97	100	113
Dalat	—	49	55	85	78	86	106
Rach Gia	—	37	50	61	81	104	100
Bien Hoa	—	38	50	83	—	177	—
Long Xuyen	—	23	25	47	73	101	—
Khanh Hung	—	40	50	52	75	75	—
Phan Thiet	—	—	—	—	80	—	—
Ban Me Thuot	—	—	—	—	64	—	—
Sa Dec	—	—	—	—	48	—	—
Phu Cuong	—	—	—	—	34	—	—
Bac Lieu	—	—	—	—	16	—	—

  * Most of these figures are based on estimates that rely on population and household surveys in these towns, not census results.

  † Figures for 1955, and 1974 to early 1975 are very broad estimates indeed.

  Source: Pressat (1974); Nguyen Duc Nhuan (1977, 1984b).

extensive war damage in the North. To add to these severe difficulties, the problem of population distribution in Vietnam *as a whole* now had to be faced (see Fig. 4.2). The problem as it presented itself to the leaders of the Socialist Republic was to try to even out some of the greatest population density differentials, especially those between the North and the South. The principal investment was to be in a series of population movements. As has been noted in Chapter 6, large-scale population resettlement movements had already become enshrined as a major (and largely successful) part of Vietnamese policy, principally as a way of dealing with the problem of too little food and too much population. However, to this vital

Table 8.3 Urban population in South Vietnam, 1943–84.

Year	Total population	Urban population of S. Vietnam	Ho Chi Minh City (agglomeration)	Ho Chi Minh City (agglomeration) as % urban population	Ho Chi Minh City (town) as % urban population	Two-city primacy index (agglomeration)	Two-city primacy index (town)	Four-city primacy index (agglomeration)	Four-city primacy index (town)
1943	—	—	498 143	—	—	—	—	—	—
1949	—	—	1 400 000	—	—	—	—	—	—
1952	—	—	1 600 970	—	—	—	—	—	—
1954	—	—	1 723 360	—	—	—	—	—	—
1956	12 670 000	—	—	—	—	—	—	—	—
1958	12 953 000	2 130 000	—	—	—	—	—	—	—
1960	14 072 000	2 815 000	2 296 000	81.6	49.7	22.0	13.5	8.9	5.4
1964	15 715 000	4 086 000	2 431 000	59.5	39.1	16.3	10.7	7.5	4.9
1968	17 414 000	6 269 000	3 156 000	50.3	26.8	9.4	5.0	5.2	2.7
1971	18 758 000	8 010 000	3 500 000	43.7	22.5	7.9	4.1	4.2	2.2
1974	—	—	4 000 000	—	—	8.0	3.7	4.2	2.2
1975 (April)	—	—	4 500 000(?)	—	—	—	—	—	—
1976	22 696 000	6 805 000	3 460 500	50.8	—	—	—	—	—
1979*	25 477 394†	6 667 242	3 419 978	51.3	—	10.7	8.5	4.9	3.9
1984	—	—	3 293 146	—	—	—	—	—	—

* Year of census. All other figures are based on estimates from surveys.
† In 1979 new administrative boundaries were drawn and the South was redefined omitting two of its former provinces and 52742 people.
Sources: Burchett (1956), Ng Shui Meng (1974), Nguyen Thy (1974), Goodman & Franks (1975), Turley (1975b), Nguyen Duc Nhuan (1977, 1984b), Fraser (1981, 1985), Monnier (1981), *Vietnam Courier* (1983, 1985).

imperative were now added two other motivations: the problems of the Southern cities and defence. Post-reunification population movements must be seen as the composite result of these three driving forces.

In so far as Figure 6.1 and the available data in Table 6.1 allow us to deduce, the North continued in the régime of *slow urban growth* throughout the period from 1975–6 to 1982. In contrast, in the South the period from April 1975 to about 1980 (Table 8.3) was one of rapid *de-urbanization* with a series of attacks on the middle class typical of the type described in the Murray and Szelenyi (1984) model. From about 1980, however, there appeared to be signs of the beginning of a régime of *slow urban growth* as the Socialist Republic began to claw its way out of the turmoil caused by the incorporation of the South. However, it is still too early, even in 1985, to make any definitive judgements.

Slow urban growth in the north, 1975–6 to 1985

In the North, urban growth remained relatively slow. There were a number of reasons for this state of affairs of which four stand out during this period. First, war damage and the diversion of funds to war hampered urban (and related industrial) development. Thus the rebuilding of the bomb-damaged cities continued,[2] but there was a general lack of funds available for redevelopment which made this rebuilding problematic. Further, cement was in continual short supply.[3] A major emphasis therefore was put on the construction of small cement mills by the government in order to overcome shortages which were, in turn, partly caused by the war damage to the Haiphong and other cement factories (see Nguyen Tien Hung 1977, *Far Eastern Economic Review* 1978). In the North, and in the Socialist Republic as a whole, however, house building seems to have been given a low priority, especially after 1978 (see Table 8.4) when it took a second place to defence construction. The 1978 plan had envisaged construction of 4 million m^2 of housing, but only 1.5 million m^2 were actually built. Only 1 million m^2 were built in 1979 (*Far Eastern Economic Review* 1980). Although house construction has increased again since the war years, at present "the average city dweller still has only 2.5 metres of floorspace" (*Vietnam Courier* 1982e, p. 24).

Table 8.4 Housing construction in the Socialist Republic of Vietnam: some indirect indicators.

	1976	1977	1978	1979	1980
per capita output of cement (kg)	15.0	16.8	16.3	14.1	11.9
state investment in housing (million dongs)	88.6	143.6	165.0	103.7	76.0
% state investment in housing	3.0	4.0	4.3	2.8	2.1

Source: Socialist Republic of Vietnam (1981).

Secondly, and related to the first point, industrial development was slow and erratic, with only a few selected large-scale industrial projects being completed. What industrial growth there was mainly occurred, partly by default and partly by design, in the more decentralized handicrafts sector.

Thirdly, it can be assumed that attempts continued in the North to create a more balanced urban system (see Ch. 6). But, as Table 6.1 shows, and allowing for boundary changes in 1979, the primacy of Hanoi (at least when measured in terms of percentage population residing in Hanoi against total urban population) seems to have remained at about the same level throughout the period.

Finally, population resettlement programmes continued to operate (Jones & Fraser 1982). As before, the object was mainly to reduce rural population densities in the Red River Delta and Northern Plains provinces. Most internal movement was to the highlands bordering China (Fig. 8.1) and, undoubtedly, part of the reason for this movement was defence. However, with reunification, a new option was opened up in the form of resettlement in the South and full advantage was taken of this option (see below).

One further important population movement with undoubted impacts on Northern urban growth should be mentioned. During 1978 and 1979 some 261 000 ethnic Chinese left North Vietnam, mainly for China, as a result of new clampdowns on free market activity and the climate of tension caused by the general background of war (see Woodside 1979). Many of these Chinese were undoubtedly urban traders from Hanoi and Haiphong who were the subject of a campaign that pre-dated and may well have set the scene for the 1978 campaign in the South. In Haiphong, for example, the city's:

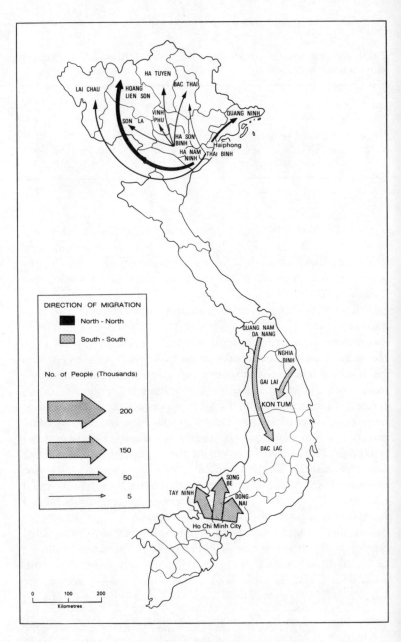

Figure 8.1 Projected population movements North–North and South–South in the Socialist Republic of Vietnam 1976–80.
Source: Jones and Fraser (1982), p. 122, from *Nhan Dan*, January 12, 1977.

1.2 million people include important numbers of overseas Chinese. Despite the superficial collectivisation of Haiphong businesses by 1960, private traders and the 'free market' still accounted for 32 per cent of the retail commerce in this city in 1974. To curb the growing private marketing activities in Haiphong, the Vietnamese government by its own admission in 1977 smashed thousands of houses, huts and merchandising stands which had been 'illegally' erected in the inner and outer cities, and sent thousands of Haiphong's unauthorized small traders to four specially created work camps (Woodside 1979, p. 404).

De-urbanization in the South, 1975–6 to 1980

There can be no doubt that de-urbanization took place in the South on a drastic and lasting scale. It is possible to isolate three main imperatives that lay behind this de-urbanization. First, there was an *economic–practical* imperative. The Southern cities, as has been shown above, were swollen by refugees. Some cities had been damaged in the war, a few extensively. Even worse, the cities had been torn away from the economy of the United States, upon which they depended to varying degrees. The result was that the Southern cities could not support urban population on the former scale. Secondly, there was an *economic–internal security* imperative. The Southern urban middle class threatened the existence of the Northern state and state class by undermining the dictates of centralized planning, and the cities were full of ex-employees of the Republic of Vietnam and ex-soldiers of the Army of the Republic of Vietnam (ARVN). Finally, there was a *moral* imperative. The Southern cities were symbols of all of the iniquities of capitalism. Nguyen Khac Vien (1982a, p. 22) expresses this strand of puritanical concern well:

Is (Ho Chi Minh) city to become a parasitic metropolis, a consumer society, a colossal leech that will suck up the nation's wealth for its orgies and revelries, or is it to become an industrial, scientific, cultural and international relations centre for the whole of the Mekong delta, a pole of development whose activity will benefit the whole country?

The economic–practical imperative manifested itself immediately in two ways. First, there were the immediate effects of the war to be contended with. About 9000 of the approximately 15 000 rural villages in the South had been damaged or destroyed during the Second Indochina War and millions of people were driven into the Southern cities. (In the South as a whole one (inflated) estimate is that in 1975 there were 600 000 war orphans, several hundred thousand war widows, 400 000 invalided war cripples, 3 million unemployed, 600 000 prostitutes and even 500 000 drug addicts; Socialist Republic of Vietnam 1980, Westing 1983). Secondly, there was the problem of rebuilding urban economies in such a way that they no longer depended upon their "consumer town aspect" (see Dao Van Tap 1980) but could still support considerable urban populations. The answers to these problems were twofold and consisted of large-scale population movements and some attempts at integrated urban planning in order to produce a productive urban base.

The population movements started almost immediately. At first, many of them were informal, consisting simply of refugees streaming back to their home villages, but by 1976 a formal plan of movement of people out of the Southern cities to inhabit the New Economic Zones in the less populated areas had been initiated as part of a more general plan of movement in the Socialist Republic as a whole. Three different streams of movement were envisaged in this general plan. First, there was movement internal to the North. Secondly, there was an internal Southern programme which consisted, in the main, of de-urbanization. Thus, in the 1976–80 Five Year Plan, 45 000 people were initially planned to be moved from Da Nang and a further 370 000 from Ho Chi Minh City (Fig. 8.1). Most of the population was to be moved relatively short distances to the provinces immediately to the north of Ho Chi Minh City. Thirdly, there was a programme to move massive numbers of North Vietnamese from the Northern rural provinces to the South (Fig. 8.2). Part of the reason for the destinations of these moves was undoubtedly "strategic".[4] Thus many were sent to the provinces adjoining the Cambodian border where their presence may well have contributed to the causes of the war with Cambodia. Others were sent to the Central Highlands where they must have had the useful effect of providing a loyal population in the middle of some troublesome mountain tribes. Yet others were sent to the Southern coastal areas. In all, a target figure of 4 million was set for population movements in the 1976–80 planning period (Jones & Fraser

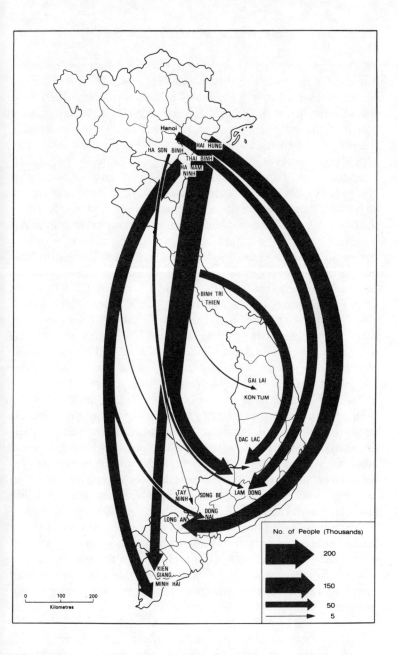

Figure 8.2 Projected population movements North–South in the Socialist Republic of Vietnam, 1976–80.
  Source: Jones and Fraser (1982), p. 122, from *Nhan Dan*, January 12, 1977.

1982). However, in reality, only about 1.5 million people were moved. Of those that moved, about 40% (600 000) moved from North to South. Many fewer than 1 million were therefore moved from towns in the South into the countryside. To make matters worse, as many as 30% of those displaced to the countryside returned to the towns and cities (Nguyen Duc Nhuan 1984b).

In the period 1981–6, nothing daunted, a figure for population movement of 3–4 million was targeted. The primary aim of the plan was to move 10 million people from the North to the South by the year 2000, thus avoiding the need to move food from the South to the North. A subsidiary aim and an ambitious one given continuing population growth was "to hold the size of the cities in the south constant" (Jones & Fraser 1982, p. 126). As of 1985, however, this programme of population movement was also running seriously behind schedule. In the four years from 1981 to 1984, 921 000 people were actually moved in the Socialist Republic as a whole (*Indochina Chronology* 1985, 4(1), p. 6) to the New Economic Zones and elsewhere. In the first quarter of 1985 a further 74 798 people were moved to the New Economic Zones (*Indochina Chronology* 1985, 4(2), p. 6). However, there was also a continuing flow of people back to the towns and cities to contend with.

Attempts at integrated urban planning were also made, nearly all of them with the aim of increasing the ability of the Southern cities to produce rather than consume. The immediate practical steps included the development of the cities' "suburbs" as food-producing areas, the collectivization of industry, and so on. However, longer-term steps were also taken. For example, there were plans to develop, over the course of "two or three" five-year plans, existing small towns and villages so as to produce a more even urban hierarchy. It was argued that most small towns in the South had a very limited rôle based on government administration rather than production of goods. Dao Van Tap's exposition of these plans is heavy with themes that can just as easily be found in the literature on small towns that is one of the darlings of current development planning practice:

The time has come to enlarge and redevelop these towns, to turn them into areas of several thousand inhabitants, with all the characteristics of economic, political and cultural centres. Several industrial plants will be built . . ., as well as trade and shopping facilities and communication links within the district and outside it . . .

The towns . . . evenly distributed in hundreds of districts throughout the country, will be key elements in the bid to lessen the gap between urban and rural ways of life.

A provision of small towns next to a reasonable number of medium size and large towns will enable the country to avoid or considerably reduce a whole series of acute social problems attendant on the creation of large cities and agglomerations.

Such plans as these have now been merged into the programme of building up the district as an important administrative and productive unit. In the Socialist Republic as a whole it is now envisaged that the population will eventually be concentrated in some 400 district towns, each accommodating about 200 000 people. (*Indochina Chronology* 1985, 4(1), p. 4).

The economic–internal security imperative manifested itself in the series of attacks on the urban middle class related in Chapter 7. Many of the urban middle class were ethnic Chinese who were particularly singled out. To begin with, their treatment stemmed from a general anti-Chinese sentiment (see Woodside 1979). Later, the Third Indochina War fuelled that resentment. However, the urban middle class ethnic Chinese were certainly not the only social group who incurred the new régime's displeasure. There were also groups like the Catholics, the Buddhists, the Hoa-Hao and the Cao-Dai. Then there were all the ex-employees of the Republic of Vietnam[5] and the many ex-soldiers of the ARVN.[6] Thayer (1982) estimated the size of forces of the Republic of Vietnam at 1.1 million soldiers in 1975. This figure does not take into account 125 000 police and 350 000 associated civil servants. Many people were simultaneously members of more than one of these groupings and were therefore under particular suspicion.

Clearly members of these groupings must have figured disproportionately amongst those chosen to leave the relative comfort of the Southern cities for a more spartan life in the New Economic Zones.[7] Even more importantly perhaps, it is these groupings that have formed the bulk of the refugees that have left Vietnam (Table 8.5). These refugees constitute a *vital* component of recent population movements in Vietnam (Figs. 8.3 and 8.4). By the end of 1982 it was estimated that 700 000 refugees had departed from Vietnam

Table 8.5   The outflow of recorded refugees from the Socialist Republic of Vietnam, 1977–82.

Countries of temporary asylum	1977	1978	1979	1980	1981	1982
Australia	861	747	497	—	30	—
Brunei	38	35	—	29	—	—
China	—	—	70	220	54	—
Hong Kong	1007	NA★	72 020	11 170	8475	2271
Indonesia	679	NA	48 651	6821	9328	1963
Japan	851	722	NA	1278	1026	214
Korea	161	98	150	20	168	—
Macau	25	945	3350	2270	448	2
Malaysia	5817	63 120	53 996	18 263	23 113	6719
Philippines	1153	2582	7821	4932	8353	711
Singapore	308	1828	5451	9280	9381	321
Thailand	4536	6325	11 928	21 549	18 378	3642
other	221	464	372	1	—	—
subtotal (boat people)	15 657	88 736	205 489	75 833	78 754	15 843
Thailand (land people)	31 214	61 662	65 393	43 569	24 414	3006
grand total (boat and land)	46 871	150 398	270 882	119 402	103 168	18 849
cumulative total	46 871	197 269	468 151	587 553	690 721	709 570

★NA, not available.
Source: United Nations High Commissioner for Refugees (various dates).

since reunification,[8] at least a third of whom were ethnic Chinese (see Pike 1982, Subcommittee of Immigrant and Refugee Affairs 1982, Thayer 1982, Rogge 1985). The outflow still continues although now on a more ordered basis under the Orderly Departure Scheme. For example in 1984 it was reported that there were about 30 000 legal departures under the Orderly Departure Scheme from Vietnam, compared to 1979 in 1979, 6598 in 1980, 11 212 in 1981, 11 147 in 1982 and 19 494 in 1983. Illegal departures, by contrast, were estimated, in both 1983 and 1984, at 24 000 (*Indochina Chronology* 1984 3(1), p. 3 & 3(4), p. 7). In total, then, almost 54 000 people still departed from Vietnam as late as 1984.

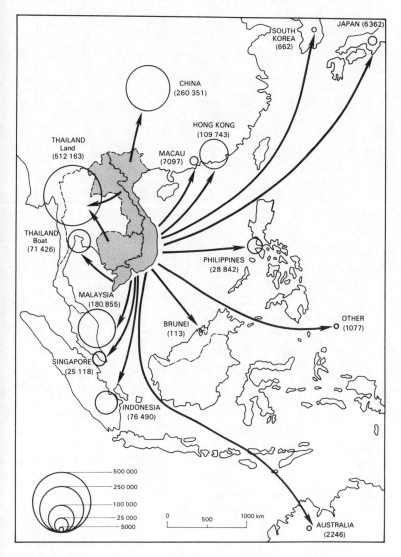

Figure 8.3 The first country of asylum of Indochinese refugees, 1976–82. *Source*: Rogge (1985), p. 68.

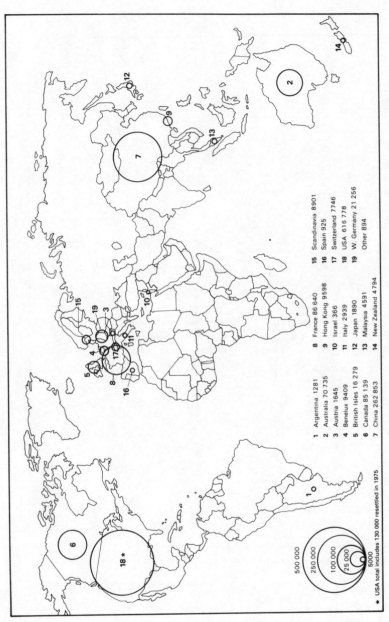

Figure 8.4 The countries of permanent resettlement of Indochinese refugees, 1976–82.
Source: Rogge (1985), p. 70.

1 Argentina 1281
2 Australia 70 735
3 Austria 1645
4 Benelux 9409
5 British Isles 16 279
6 Canada 85 139
7 China 262 853
8 France 86 640
9 Hong Kong 9598
10 Israel 366
11 Italy 2939
12 Japan 1890
13 Malaysia 4591
14 New Zealand 4794
15 Scandinavia 8901
16 Spain 925
17 Switzerland 7746
18 USA 616 778
19 W. Germany 21 256
Other 894

500 000
250 000
100 000
25 000
5000

* USA total includes 130 000 resettled in 1975

Finally, there was the moral imperative. The cities had to be transformed into containers of socialist thought. This meant the "re-education" of former military and some government personnel. Initially, somewhere between 60 000 and 200 000 such personnel were required to undergo extensive re-education in camps. The exact number still in camps is a matter of dispute, especially since many of those now in camps were put there *after* the original post-war period of re-education (Marr 1982). Estimates range from the official figure of 10 000 upwards.[9] The moral imperative also meant that those not chosen for a period of re-education in the camps were still exposed to socialization in unions, women's groups, and so on. In the cities, people were organized into solidarity groups of about 50 families. These groups are linked hierarchically to higher administrative levels (see Ch. 4).

The data do not exist to make it possible to give a grand accounting of all the different population movements that had an impact on the population of the Southern cities – the formal (and informal) population movements, the people leaving the country, the people in re-education camps, and so on. However, enough data exist from census sources for the Republic of Vietnam and the Socialist Republic to show the cumulative impacts to 1979. By this date Ho Chi Minh City had certainly undergone a drastic period of de-urbanization (Table 8.6).[10] Nevertheless, the problem of the primacy of Ho Chi Minh City in the Southern urban system had not been solved. To take just the most commonly used measure of primacy, the two–city index, it appears that Ho Chi Minh City was eight times larger than Da Nang, the second largest city, in 1974, but nearly 11 times larger in 1979. The four–city index shows a situation nearer to equilibrium. Of course, these figures do not tell us anything about developments further down the urban hierarchy, but Table 8.3 shows that the population of Ho Chi Minh City as a percentage of urban population stayed constant through the process of reunification; certainly, it did not decrease.

Part of the reason for this state of affairs was, of course, that de-urbanization was even more dramatic in many other Southern cities (Fig. 8.5 & Table 8.6). Thus Da Nang, Hue and Quy Nhon each lost more than 20% of their population in the 1974–9 period. Other cities such as Can Tho remained stable, and Long Xuyen and Bien Hoa actually gained some population. There were corresponding changes in the ranks of cities as a result of these population

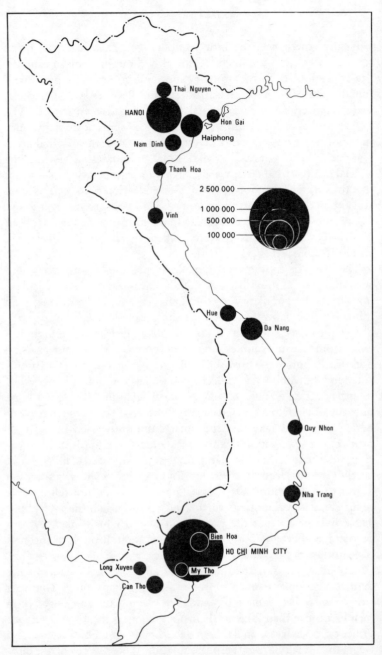

Figure 8.5 The population of the largest cities of the Socialist Republic of Vietnam, 1979 (for Hanoi, Haiphong and Ho Chi Minh City, the size of the circle refers to the town rather than the agglomeration population).
Source: United Nations Fund for Population Activities (1981).

Table 8.6 Population decreases in South Vietnamese cities, 1974 and 1979.*

	1974	1979	Absolute change 1974–9	% change 1974–9	Change in rank 1974–5
Ho Chi Minh City (agglomeration)	4 000 000	3 419 978	−580 022	−14.5	1–1
Da Nang	500 000	318 655	−181 345	−32.7	2–2
Bien Hoa	177 000†	190 086	+13 086	+ 7.4	7–3
Can Tho	180 000	182 856	+2856	+ 1.6	6–4
Nha Trang	200 000	172 663	−27 337	−16.7	5–5
Hue	210 000	165 865	−44 135	−21.1	4–6
Quy Nhon	240 000	130 534	−109 466	−45.6	3–7
Long Xuyen	101 000†	112 488	+11 488	+11.4	9–8
My Tho	120 000	101 469	−18 531	−15.5	8–9
Two-city primacy index	8.0 (3.7)‡	10.7 (8.5)			
Four-city primacy index	4.6 (2.2)	4.9 (3.9)			

* 1974 figures are estimates. Higher figures for 1974 are given from North Vietnamese sources for Da Nang and Nha Trang by Nguyen Duc Nhuan (1977). 1979 figures are from the Census of that year for the Socialist Republic of Vietnam.

† 1971 figures.

‡ Figures in brackets are indices calculated on urban rather than agglomeration totals.

Source: Nguyen Duc Nhuan (1977), United Nations Fund for Population Activities (1981).

changes: Bien Hoa moved to third place from seventh, Hue fell from fourth to sixth place, and Quy Nhon from third to seventh. It is noticeable that it is the northern Southern cities that have lost most population whereas, on the whole, the southern Southern cities have gained population or stabilized. An important reason for these population changes, as least after the immediate exodus at the ending of the Second Indochina War, was the state of the economy of the different groups of cities. The northern Southern cities had fallen on hard times.[11] The southern Southern cities, with their rich agricultural hinterlands, were more able to support large populations in the changed circumstances after reunification. These cities have also been a focus for many of the population movements from the North and some of the short-term movements from Ho Chi Minh City.

The composite figures do, of course, conceal what may well be much greater in-movements and out-movements for which there are no data. They also conceal the changes in the social composition of many of the Southern cities that must have come about as a result of the exodus of the ethnic Chinese and other social groupings, and the arrival of Northern cadres. Some of this detail will be brought out for Ho Chi Minh City in Chapter 9.

Slow urban growth in the South, 1980–5

It is still too early to make any convincing judgements but it is possible to suggest that by around 1980 the Southern cities were slipping into a régime of slow urban growth similar to that already found in the North. The population of Ho Chi Minh City has continued to decrease marginally since 1980 (Table 8.3)[12] but the most traumatic period of de-urbanization now seems to be over. Some Southern cities, such as Hue, seem to have gained quite dramatically in population (Shaplen 1985b); others, like Da Nang (with 350 000 people in 1984), have now stabilized their population.[13]

Notes

1   Rogge (1985) gives a figure of 65% for the urban population as a proportion of total population of the South in early 1975. Even given the events of that year this figure seems unlikely.

2   One source (Socialist Republic of Vietnam 1980) estimates that 5 million m^2 of dwelling houses were destroyed in the North as a result of the Second Indochina War. The situation was only exacerbated by the Chinese incursion into the Northern provinces. The major point of destruction was "the town of Long An, fifteen kilometres from the border. Buildings not destroyed in artillery duels were methodically demolished with TNT by Chinese units prior to departure" (Marr 1982, p. 59). Another five major towns were also badly damaged (Shaplen 1985b).

3   Cement continues to be in short supply, even with the addition of four new cement factories producing more than a million tons per year. The five-year goal is for a fourfold increase (Shaplen 1985a, p. 122).

4   Nguyen Duc Nhuan (1984b, p. 321) cites a passage from *Tap Chi Cong San*, the journal of the Vietnamese Communist Party, which confirms this interpretation. See Chapter 10.

5   Numbering over 1 million people. Most of these were enfranchised,

but the higher up personnel were "re-educated". The priority categories for re-education were the following: elected officials; civil servants with the rank of director or above; members of political parties; members of the Rural Development Corps and Operation "Phoenix"; police officers with the rank of second lieutenant and above; religious leaders.

6   Again, not all of the ARVN could have been clapped in irons. Priority categories for "re-education" were: officers with the rank of second lieutenant and above; NCOs from political warfare, intelligence, the Special Forces, the airborne and the marines; NCOs from the police field forces and the Special Police.

7   Unfortunately, there are no figures on the social composition of those sent to the zones.

8   Not all the refugees were from the South, of course. Many Chinese, mentioned above, left from the North as did peasants. Nor were all the refugees from social groupings under suspicion. Some left simply to escape the poverty. A constant experience in Vietnam is being asked to take letters to family and friends now overseas.

9   See Nguyen Van Canh (1983) for a useful survey of the estimates available.

10 It is vital to remember that the figures in Table 8.6 *do not show the true extent of de-urbanization*, most particularly because during the period from 1974 to 1979 the birth rate was still 2.6% but also because they provide no clue to the extent of in-movements to and out-movements from the Southern cities.

11 Da Nang still has the highest unemployment rate in Vietnam.

12 It is not known whether the figures for urban population given by the Socialist Republic include the population that drifted back from the New Economic Zones. If not, then this could make a considerable difference to the figures for some cities.

13 Clearly birth control must be a vital element in any serious population policy for Vietnam. Yet most commentators on Vietnamese family planning (e.g. United Nations Fund for Population Activities 1978, 1981; Fraser 1979, 1985; Jones & Fraser 1982; *Far Eastern Economic Review* 1984; Nguyen Duc Nhuan 1984b; Shaplen 1985a) seem to agree that the Vietnamese effort in this direction is still curiously half-hearted. The official target for population growth is 1.7% per annum. Vietnam has come nowhere near reaching this target as yet and seems quite unlikely to do so in the near future. In 1984, for example, the population growth rate was 2.23% (*Indochina Chronology* 1985, 4(2), p. 5), although birth rates were generally lower in the cities (Nguyen Duc Nhuan 1984b, Fraser 1985).

9 *A tale of two cities: the experiences of Hanoi and Saigon (Ho Chi Minh City) under socialist rule*

So far, the discussion of urbanization under socialism in the North and South of Vietnam has remained largely synoptic. In this chapter, in contrast, an attempt is made to crystallize out some of the more general observations that have been made in the previous chapters in the context of the experience of particular cities. The cities that have been chosen are Hanoi since the advent of the Democratic Republic of Vietnam in 1954 and Ho Chi Minh City since the reunification of 1975. Clearly neither city can be regarded as "typical" of urbanization under socialism – real places are not like that – but many of the themes of Chapters 5, 6, 7 and 8 will re-appear in their histories, although now tied to the concrete circumstances of particular contexts (Thrift 1983).

Hanoi, 1945–85

Hanoi was chosen as the capital of North Vietnam in 1010 but did not get its modern name until 1831 (Socialist Republic of Vietnam 1979). In 1882 the city was taken over by the French and became, with the nearby part city of Haiphong, the centre of French colonial operations in Northern Indochina (Robequain 1944, Murray 1980). In time, the city came to have a sizeable number of wage-labourers, concentrated in industries like textiles, brewing, soap and cigarette making, and chemicals. Wages in the city were kept low by a continual influx of landless villagers who formed something of an underclass, living in squalid slums.

On September 2, 1945, Ho Chi Minh read the Declaration of Independence in Hanoi, founding a Democratic Republic. However, independence did not last for long. The city was brought low by the effects of the struggle against French occupying forces.

In two months of fighting between 19 December 1946 and 17 February 1947, all of the city's essential services and most of its industry were destroyed. In addition to insecurity and hardships caused by the fighting, urban life was made almost unbearable by an absence of grain reserves (due to an earlier famine throughout the North) and severance of access to agricultural areas by French encirclement. The civilian population not only had a strong motivation to leave the city but also burdened the forces that remained . . . When the fighting ended people were reluctant to return because of delayed restoration of services, destruction of homes, lack of commerce and capital, exorbitant costs of living and patriotic distaste at the idea of returning to a zone of French control. In 1948–49, Hanoi's population may have been as low as 10,000 . . . (Turley 1975b, p. 371).

Although the French were subsequently able to take control of the city – from February 1947 to May 1954 – they failed to build up the small industrial base destroyed in the events of 1946–7. Instead, from 1949 to 1950 they grossly expanded the city's commercial, service and administrative functions and, in what was almost a dress rehearsal for the later American presence in Saigon, created a service and supply economy heavily dependent upon France. The existence of this type of inflated urban economy had three main effects. First, it attracted substantial migration into the city, most especially by formerly resident small-business men in 1948–9 and thereafter by persons who had not previously resided in the city. By 1952 the city's population was more than twice its pre-war size. Secondly, Hanoi's economy became substantially reliant on external supply, not only from France but also from South Vietnam (70–80% of Hanoi's rice came from the Saigon area). Thirdly, as is the way with service and supply economies, the need for consumer goods and services rapidly produced numerous small retailers. By mid-1954, about 40 000 market stallholders, shopkeepers, pedlars and sidewalk hawkers serviced a metropolitan area population of 380 000–400 000. One family in every two relied on this informal sector to survive.[1]

On taking over the reins of power in Hanoi in October 1954, the city government[2] installed by the new Republic was therefore confronted with an economy cut off from its *raison d'être*: France. In late 1954 Hanoi had a industrial sector consisting of only eight small, privately owned factories (and nine other factories that had been dismantled and moved out of the city to the resistance zones and which were now moved back in; see Duiker 1981) plus 496 small private machine shops, all poorly equipped and operating erratically owing to the general scarcity of raw materials. Unemployment stood at 77 000 or about one-fifth of the city's population (an unemployment rate of 30% at least). Of those employed, only 5000 were members of an industrial working class. In contrast, a further 7600 were stallholders, 10 000 were shop owners, 10 000 were pedlars and another 10 000 were sidewalk hawkers. Added to this, there were some 15 000 prostitutes and 19 000 abandoned children (see Turley 1975b, *Vietnam Courier* 1982e). There were some advantages to weigh up against these disadvantages, however. First, as was pointed out in Chapter 6, the exodus to the South of the (few) capitalists, the more prosperous elements amongst the petty bourgeoisie and the Catholics, meant that there was little opposition to the régime. The petty bourgeoisie that remained were of much too recent origin to constitute a closely knit social class. Secondly, some of the population of Hanoi in October 1954 were undoubtedly refugees, only too pleased to return home. Thirdly, there was a reservoir of administrative skills amongst the *indigénes* of the former French civil service waiting to be tapped in order to help govern the city.[3]

In the period of slow urban growth from 1954 to 1965 (during which time Hanoi grew more rapidly than any other city, increasing its primacy considerably in the country's urban system), the policies of the new government of Hanoi were threefold. First, the industrial sector had to be built up. Following two years of "economic rehabilitation" in 1956 and 1957 (during which time private production was allowed to increase by 272% in order to reduce unemployment), Hanoi took its part in the Three Year Plan (1958–60) to socialize existing industry and build new industry. Thus 495 existing enterprises owned by 403 "capitalists" were re-organized into 62 joint state-private and 16 co-operative enterprises. By 1960 5027 workers (45% of the total in former private enterprise) were employed in state-owned enterprises. The collectivization of small industries and handicrafts was also all but completed by 1960. Ninety-five per cent of the craftsmen joined production or service co-operatives, and 926 production co-operatives accounted for 50% of the total workforce. In the informal sector 27 344 small traders were organized into 2266 co-operatives of various forms, and a further 2534 switched to handicraft production. The larger merchants were made agents of the State Trading Corporation or compelled to share ownership with the state. In addition to the socialization of existing industry, new industry was also built up, often on the outskirts of the city (*Vietnam Courier* 1982e).

By 1964 another 99 state-owned enterprises had been built to add to the 17 large enterprises that existed in late 1954, including the Hanoi Mechanical Engineering Plant (now the Hanoi Machine Tool Plant No. 1), the first large state-built factory, opened in 1957 (and funded from Soviet aid). By 1965, another 78 joint state-private and co-operative enterprises along with 928 small-industry and handicraft co-operatives had been organized in Hanoi (*Vietnam Courier* 1982e).

Secondly, now that the lifeline to the South had been cut off, the city had to feed itself. Agriculture was the priority. As in Cuba in later years (see Gugler 1978), the city's "suburbs" were made the focus of an intensive campaign to increase productivity by planting more vegetables and other staples. The agriculture sector was also socialized. By 1960, 88% of peasant families in the four suburban districts of Tu Liem, Thanh Tri, Gia Lam and Dong Anh had joined co-operatives. By 1974 more than 317 high-level co-operatives had been set up. From 1961 to 1964 nine state farms were also established (*Vietnam Courier* 1982e).

Thirdly, the city's administration had to be revamped. In 1960, the boundaries of the city were extended (partly to enable all the city's major food-growing areas to be in its control). The city itself was organized on the classical socialist system of wards, blocks and cells, with the ward being the lowest level of administrative authority. The number of wards was gradually reduced from 36 in 1959, to 12 in 1958, to eight in 1954 and to four in 1961 (Turley 1975b).[4]

At first, the war did not affect Hanoi, but on February 28, 1965, after major American air strikes in the North earlier in the month, the order was given to evacuate children and old people. Approximately 50 000 people were removed by the autumn. Following Operation "Rolling Thunder" in April 1966, only the indispensable were allowed to remain in the city. Artisans, teachers, small shopkeepers, children and day labourers all had to leave (Turley 1975b). Probably a further one-third to one half of the population left at this time (Fig. 9.1). Governmental agencies were relocated up to 65 km outside the city, factories were dismantled and relocated, even many handicraft industries were moved as the bombing continued. By early 1968 the maximum degree of evacuation had been reached (Fig. 9.1). Although bombing was restricted to areas south of the 20th parallel in April 1968, the government continued to discourage movement back into the city until the bombing halt of November 1, 1968. At this point many evacuees returned to the city so that by 1972 the city's population had climbed to 1.2 million, but the continued dispersal of government offices and factories meant that many other evacuees were forced to remain outside the city.

When bombing was resumed on April 17, 1972, the city's population was rapidly evacuated again (Fig. 9.1). First to go were 30 000 women and children. Once again, numerous production facilities not already operating outside the city limits were decentralized. This second round of evacuations eventually proved to be on a greater scale than that of the 1960s (in that more people had to be removed from a higher population figure). Somewhere between 550 000 and 720 000 persons were evacuated – up to 60% of the agglomeration and up to 75% of the inner city population (Turley 1975b). The scale of the evacuation was such that it eventually caused considerable problems in administering the city. In the end, state and party cadres had to be assigned to run blocks, a level of administration usually left to popular participation. Inevitably, this expansion of the state to the lower levels of administration taxed already widely spread administrative skills (especially since so many cadres were fighting in the war). However, the bombing of Operation "Linebacker II" in December 1972 was serious enough to cause even further evacuations, spurred on by the high casualty figures: 2196 people were killed and 1577 wounded in these attacks (Turley 1975b).

It is not surprising, then, that on the cessation of the bombing in 1973, Hanoi was left in disarray. The city, it seemed, could *not* be immediately re-occupied by all of its former population:

The most serious obstacle to immediate reoccupation of the city was the shortage of housing. One of the first damage assess-

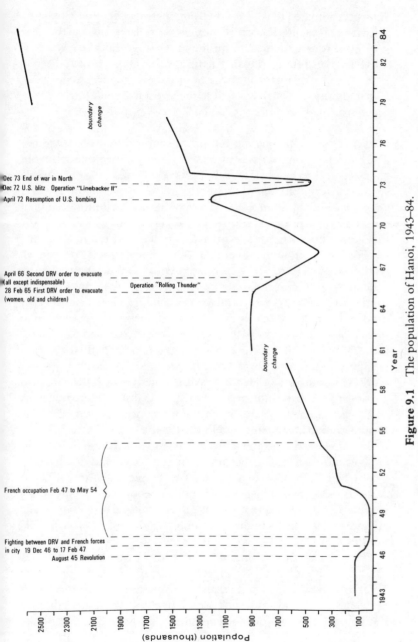

Figure 9.1 The population of Hanoi, 1943–84.

Sources: Burchett (1956), Ng Shui Meng (1974), Nguyen Thy (1974), Goodman and Franks (1975), Turley (1975b) Nguyen Duc Nhuan (1977, 1984b), Fraser (1981, 1985), Monnier (1981), *Vietnam Courier* (1983, 1985).

Text labels within the figure:

Dec 73 End of war in North
Dec 72 U.S. blitz Operation "Linebacker II"
April 72 Resumption of U.S. bombing

April 66 Second DRV order to evacuate
(all except indispensable)
28 Feb 65 First DRV order to evacuate
(women, old and children)

Operation "Rolling Thunder"

boundary change

French occupation Feb 47 to May 54

Fighting between DRV and French forces
in city 19 Dec 46 to 17 Feb 47
August 45 Revolution

Population (thousands)

Year

ments estimated that 17,000 housing units had been destroyed, leaving 'tens of thousands' homeless. A later survey found 215,000 square metres of housing in the three inner city wards of Hai Bai Trung, (Hoan Kiem) and Ba Dinh to have been destroyed or damaged, and a Soviet correspondent reported that almost one quarter of all living space in Hanoi (including suburbs) had been destroyed (Turley 1975b, pp. 388–9).

However, many people did (return,) causing severe overcrowding. The burden on the city was increased by the inflow of people from places other than Hanoi (Fig. 8.1, Table 6.1). Indeed, the burden was so great that the city did not return to anything resembling pre-war normality until well into 1974. Disappointment with the results of the first year's reconstruction was publicly admitted. Thus in the first year, administration was often chaotic and, as a result, abnormal levels of corruption were reported. Some housing was constructed on the outskirts (but, not surprisingly) with too much haste. Large-scale industry took time to set up and get running again. Only the handicraft sector was successful in maintaining an increasing level of production and the city's 50 000–60 000 men and women who carried out handicrafts quasi-privately were encouraged to produce more (at the cost of black markets which sprang up to fill in the gaps in supply and distribution). According to the 1974 census, the active working population of Hanoi was distributed in the following proportions: 32% in the industrial sector; 13% in distribution, transport and communication; 8.5% in health and education; and 33.8% in administration (Nguyen Duc Nhuan 1984b).

By 1975 Hanoi was gradually returning to normal and by 1980 the city's economy had again become quite complex. Thus, in that year, Hanoi had "254 state-owned factories employing some 120,000 workers, 433 small industry and handicraft cooperatives employing another 122,000 workers as well as 315 agricultural cooperatives and 10 state-owned farms in the surrounding 'suburbs'" (*Vietnam Courier* 1982e, p. 25).

The city had also become much larger. By the time of the 1979 census, the population had increased, with the aid of a major boundary re-organization, to more than three-quarters of a million people in the inner city and a further 1½ million in the whole city administrative area,[5] making for a total population of more than 2¼ million. By 1984 the population had increased again, this time to an overall total of 2 674 000, with 826 900 people living in the inner city and another 1 847 500 living in the city area as a whole (*Vietnam Courier* 1985) (Fig. 9.2 & Table 9.1).

However, the legacy of the Second Indochina War has combined

Table 9.1 The population of Hanoi, 1979.

District	Area (km^2)	Population	Population density (per km^2)	Administrative arrangements
Hoan Kiem	4.5	154 000	34 222	18 wards
Dong Da	14.0	223 000	15 928	25 wards
Ba Dinh	10.5	160 700	15 304	15 wards
Hai Ba Trung	11.0	238 000	21 636	23 wards
	total	775 700		
Gia Lam	175.7	224 700	1279	31 communes and 2 townships: Gia Lam, Yen Vien★
Dong Anh	184.2	169 100	918	23 communes and 1 township: Dong Anh
Me Linh	254.9	177 100	695	22 communes and 2 townships: Phuc Yen, Xuan Hoa
Soc Son	313.3	143 200	457	23 communes
Tu Liem	109.7	179 500	1636	25 communes and 3 townships: Nghia Do, Can Giay, Cau Dien
Thanh Tri	100.2	160 300	1600	26 communes and 1 township: Van Dien
Hoai Duc	122.1	151 400	1240	27 communes
Dan Phuong	76.8	87 900	1144	15 communes and 1 township: Phung
Thach That	93.4	87 500	937	19 communes
Phuc Tho	102.5	98 900	965	22 communes
Ba Vi	543.3	207 300	381	32 communes
	total	1 686 900		
Son Tay†	14.6	33 900	2322	3 wards and 9 communes
Ha Dong†	14.7	64 200	4367	2 communes

★ Two more townships, Duc Giang and Sai Dong, are to be integrated into this district.

† Son Tay town was formerly the capital of Son Tay province. Ha Dong was formerly the capital of Ha Dong province. These two provinces were merged with Hoa Binh province in 1977 to form the present province of Ha Son Binh (see Fig. 4.6).

Source: Vietnam Courier (1982e), p. 12.

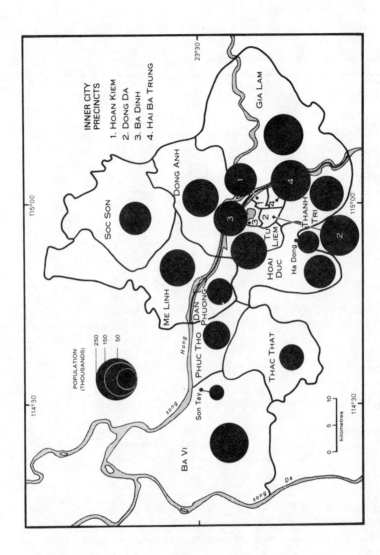

Figure 9.2 The population density of Hanoi, 1979.

with the contradictions of the Vietnamese state to leave Hanoi with considerable problems. Three of these problems are particularly important.[6] First there is still a general lack of housing space in the city. Indeed, average housing space per person decreased from 5.1 m^2 in 1954 to only 2.3 m^2 in 1982 (*Indochina Chronology* 1982, 1(2), p. 5; Nguyen Duc Nhuan 1984a):[7]

> Since 1955, no new housing has been built in Hanoi proper, though land is available and existing housing very insufficient (1.5 m^2 per person). Housing has gone up in the outskirts at 3 m^2 per person. However at least one third of the Hanoi workforce still live in rural dwellings 20 km or even 40 km from their place of work. Means of transportation are bicycles and buses (Nguyen Duc Nhuan 1984a, p. 83).

(Indeed much of Hanoi, with its often beautiful stucco colonial buildings and tree-lined avenues, exudes an air of decay, although many repairs are being carried out.)

Secondly, there are still considerable food shortages, especially of meat (*Summary of World Broadcasts* 1981, FE/W1141/A/12). An extensive free market still exists to plug the gaps. Thus:

> Dong Xuan ward on the night of the 31st May (1981) gathered all the licensed traders in the area to brief them on the policy of declaring property and goods in stock and registering and posting prices. As of 3rd June, as many as 81 per cent of the shops in the ward had completed the declaration. However, negative phenomena were still prevalent there: some families failed to declare the property and all the goods they had in stock; others, dealing in State-controlled goods, strove to hide their valuable and rare goods, so as to sell them stealthily; they displayed only ordinary goods in their showcases (*Summary of World Broadcasts* 1981, FE/W1141/A/12).

Finally, there is considerable social tension in what is still an austere and disciplined city between the wishes of the state for ideological rectitude and the desire of some of the population (especially the young) for a more colourful life, stimulated by the unification with the South and the growth of a market in consumer goods.

Both Vietnamese and Westerners told me that the mood of the

city had changed greatly in the past five or six years and . . . some of this was undoubtedly due to the influence of the South, partly because so many Northerners had served in the Army or as goverment cadremen down South or had begun to visit relatives and friends there regularly . . . 'For a while in 1978, the police would stop youngsters and tell them to go home and change their clothes or cut their hair but now the styles are pretty much accepted . . . There's an increase in consumer goods, despite many shortages, and that's what has made the difference. Television now comes right into the bedroom. Where do people get the money? By and large, farmers have done well and the workers in light industry around Hanoi are beginning to enjoy some benefits too' (Shaplen 1985a, p. 110).

Ho Chi Minh City, 1975–85

In 1861, Saigon was taken over by the French and the city then became the chief centre of French colonial operations in Southern Indochina.[8] By 1928, the population of the city (with Cholon) was already 220 000 (Socialist Republic of Vietnam 1979). The city built up a considerable industrial base founded on industries as diverse as rice milling, textiles and latterly even some assembly-line manufacturing industries (Robequain 1944, Murray 1980). In addition, the city had large and extensive port facilities. The industrial workforce was not, of course, the only element of the economically active proportion of colonial Saigon. Many people also worked in the considerable informal economy. In addition, there were rich absentee landlords from the Mekong Delta and a large number of professionals such as teachers and administrators. The social character of colonial Saigon was surprisingly diverse.

However, after the French withdrawal from Vietnam in 1954, industrial development in Saigon increasingly turned to the consumer goods sector.

With assistance from the United States and a number of other Western countries, industrial zones were established on the outskirts of Saigon and in some of the larger cities of the delta and along the central coast. Sugar refineries, pharmaceuticals, processed foods, and paper products began to appear (Duiker 1983, p. 100).

With the onset of the Second Indochina War and even greater US assistance, the consumer aspect of Saigon's economy was greatly exaggerated.

Food imports from the United States made up for chronic shortages of production in the countryside. An affluent urban middle class thrived amid a swelling urban population of poor workers, beggars and refugees flooding into refugee camps in the suburbs (Duiker 1983, p. 101).

It was into this situation that mainly northern Provisional Revolutionary Government cadres had to insert themselves in 1975. The immediate problems that the new administration of Saigon, now renamed Ho Chi Minh City, had to face were mundane but no less serious for that. For example, housing was poor and the resources for house building were limited (the average population density in the city was still 225 persons per hectare in 1981, but in some areas the figure rose to as high as 1600 persons per hectare[9]). Water and sewage drained into the river without any processing. Parts of the city were subject to flooding. The supply of electricity was insufficient and most important of all, too many food supplies had to be brought into the city, from as far away as the mountain resort town of Dalat, which could have been used for export and to generate much-needed foreign exchange (Report of Australian Committee 1981).

All of these problems were either caused or exacerbated by the city's population size, which had exploded after 1958 (Fig. 9.3). At the end of the Second Indochina War the Southern cities were crammed to overflowing with people. In Saigon there were, according to various estimates in the literature, from 3.5 million to as many as 4.5 million people in 1975. The lower figure is probably more representative of the "permanent" population (that is those who were not immediate refugees who, where possible, returned home on cessation of hostilities). Of this 3.5 million, about 1.5 million lived in slums, dependent upon the "trickle-down" effect of funds from the United States (Thayer 1982).

Immediate efforts therefore had to be made to move people out of the city. Obviously, the primary candidates were those who had been forced to evacuate their homes in the villages. However, even as early as June 1975 efforts to move people out of the city were not proving as successful as had been expected and a special conference

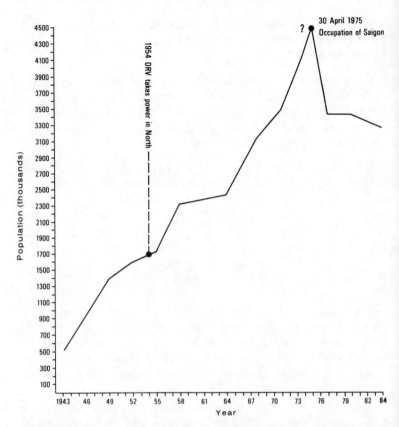

Figure 9.3 The population of Saigon/Ho Chi Minh City, 1943–84.
Sources: Burchett (1956), Ng Shui Meng (1974), Nguyen Thy (1974), Goodman and Franks (1975), Turley (1975b), Nguyen Duc Nhuan (1977, 1984b), Fraser (1981, 1985), Monnier (1981), *Vietnam Courier* (1983, 1985).

had to be called (Turley 1977a). The flow of people then increased, but successive government plans to move 1 or 1.5 million people out of Ho Chi Minh City by the end of 1976 or early 1977 produced only 227 000 departures by October 1975, 600 000 by August 1976 and 706 000 departures by April 1977. By September 1981, the city had, since liberation:

> sent 840,000 people back to their native villages or to the suburban areas and economic zones for resettlement. These people have opened up and put under cultivation tens of thousands of hectares of virgin land in various new economic zones, built 82

villages along the main highways in the eastern Nan Bo provinces, and set up 20 state farms and forestry sites around the city (*Summary of World Broadcasts* 1981, FE/W/1159/A/37).

However, by 1981 city planners were saying that it was "too difficult" to bring the population down to the target of 2.5 million that they had set themselves (see Report of Australian Committee 1981, p. 25). This was in spite of being aided by other outflows, for example of people to "re-education" camps and of refugees, many of whom came from Ho Chi Minh City. The problem was that there was also a flow of people *into* the city with at least two components. First, there were the North Vietnamese and former members of the NLF, many although not all members of the new state administrative class. Estimates vary concerning this inflow: one estimate is as high as 700 000 (Nguyen Duc Nhuan 1982b). (This is surely too high since overall migration from North to South from 1976 to 1979 was officially only 600 000; Jones 1982.) Certainly, the inflow was great enough for there now to be a policy to discourage further Northern migration into the city. Secondly:

> Thousands of people . . . clandestinely left the (New Economic Zones) and their harsh conditions to return to Ho Chi Minh City. Having lost their original homes, they lived in parks and in the streets. Western observers estimated that about 450,000 people remained unemployed (*Far Eastern Economic Review* 1981, p. 264).

(The Vietnamese official estimate of unemployment in Ho Chi Minh City in 1981 was 200 000 (Report of Australian Committee 1981). The figure is undoubtedly much higher than this now, as then.) By 1984 the city's population had decreased to 3.3 million (with 71% of the population living in the urban area and 29% in the suburbs). It is unlikely to go much below this figure.

Apart from the policy of moving people out of Ho Chi Minh City, efforts were also made to make the city's economy more self-reliant. The city's suburbs were increasingly developed as food-producing areas. In 1975, only 95 100 tonnes of rice and other cereals were produced by peasants in the suburbs. However, by 1980, this amount had increased to 200 000 tonnes, and the target for 1981 was 230 000 tonnes[10] (Report of Australian Committee 1981). By 1983, 120 000 ha of land in the city were under cultivation, a considerable increase over the 1975 figure. Plans for collectivization were well advanced. By 1983, 30 000 ha of land had been confiscated from "reactionary colonialists and landlords", and plans were made for 75% of all land under city administration to be under collective control and 85% of the peasant population collectivized by the end of 1984 (*Indochina Chronology* 1983, 3(4), p. 4). However, even with the population outflow and the extension of agricultural capacity, Ho Chi Minh City's food situation remains serious. For example, as late as 1982 Dang Duy Linh, deputy health director of Ho Chi Minh City was quoted:

> as saying that 'at least 75 per cent of the children suffer from first-degree malnutrition here' and these children attained only 80 per cent of the WHO age/weight standard. According to a study by the pediatric research centre of the number two children's hospital in Ho Chi Minh City in 1978–79, most undernourished children came from the new economic zones and rural areas . . . According to Dr. Duong Quyn Hoa, the head of the research centre, malnutrition is increasingly affecting younger children. In 1979, 15 per cent of undernourished children were under six years of age, today the figure is 24 per cent (*Summary of World Broadcasts* 1982, FE/6988/B/8/26).

The economic–internal security imperative manifested itself in Ho Chi Minh City chiefly in relation to the ownership of the city's economy (see Ch. 7). The city must have appeared to the Northern cadres and the Provisional Revolutionary Government as both a sink of capitalist iniquity and a glittering prize – in other words as a sort of Vietnamese version of Shanghai in 1949.[11] Thus:

> on the one hand, the Saigon economy offered a rather extreme model of the divorce between colonial capitalism and the interests and welfare of the indigenous lower classes; Saigon possess(ed) more than 200 hotels, and one of Southeast Asia's largest industrial capacities for producing items like laundry powder, candy bars, salad oil, cigarettes and soft drinks, many although not all of which must be sustained by foreign fuel or foreign raw material or Westernised consumer tastes. On the other hand, Saigon's concentration of modern economic assets gave Vietnamese communist managers a sort of windfall foundation for an orthodox, ideologically unadventurous

industrialisation of the country. (Saigon account(ed) for about 80 per cent of the total industrial output of the Vietnamese South in the late 1970s. Its abundance of pharmacies, lumber-processing installations, and privately-owned sewing machines, to say nothing of its strong capacities for producing bicycles, electric fans and glass, dazzled the northern revolutionaries who inherited it in the spring of 1975) (Woodside 1979, pp. 393–4).

To be more specific, Saigon employed some 200 000–300 000 workers (Nguyen Duc Nhuan 1977), mainly in small assembly and repair shops but also in a sizeable large firm sector which included, according to Cao (1978):

14 beverage companies employing close to 5000 workers;

two tobacco manufacturing companies with almost 2000 employees;

10 large textile companies with 6000 employees;

42 chemical companies with 5000 employees;

three steel companies with 2000 employees;

11 paper companies with close to 3000 workers.

Until the campaign of 1978, ownership of the industrial sector was only gradually transferred to state control (see Ch. 7). In October 1975, moves were made against the *comprador* bourgeoisie of Ho Chi Minh City:

several hundred persons (including nine key comprador bourgeoisie), many of whom were ethnic Chinese, were rounded up. Among those arrested were: Mat Hy the rice king, Luong Tu Van the fabric king, Tran Thien Hu the coffee king, Lam Hoa Ho and Ly Thong Than the scrap iron kings, Hoang An San the barbed-wire king and the Ong family which controlled textile, transport, real estate, banking and shipyards (Thayer 1982, p. 16).

It was fully expected that this limited appropriation of the high spots of the South Vietnamese economy combined with the movement of zealous cadres into management would produce an industrial boom. The reality was rather different:

in late 1975 a Liberation Trade Union official boasted that, 'once we get all the factories working full-time Ho Chi Minh City will be a very big industrial centre, the biggest in Southeast Asia'. In reality, shortages of raw materials and spare parts soon reduced the Saigon industrial workforce from 300,000 to about 150,000. The main problem was the extreme scarcity of capital with which to buy raw materials and spare parts from overseas (Marr 1982, p. 56).

A second problem was Ho Chi Minh City's 300 000 small-business men and traders, to whom some of the blame for this state of affairs was attached, along with much of the blame for the problems of co-ordination of the South Vietnamese economy. The "second battle of Saigon", launched in March 1978, was the response (see Ch. 8). The battle achieved one goal. It most certainly destroyed the power of the petty bourgeoisie of Ho Chi Minh City as a *social* class, and most especially some of its better-off ethnic Chinese elements, many of whom ultimately became refugees[12] (see Ch. 8). However, it did not achieve its economic goals. "The result of the second battle of Saigon was that the economic power of about 10 per cent of the South's private business families was annulled – a rather feeble gain for the international traumas which the commotion helped to create" (Woodside 1979, pp. 403–4). The battle did not destroy the market and it probably left the state with more problems of co-ordination than it had previously had. Further, the market was always potentially resurgent. Thus the Sixth Plenum thaw of 1979 had an almost immediate effect:

> by March 1980, according to one western eyewitness, 'these policy changes were having an effect, especially in the South. Indeed people spoke of the economy exploding . . . In Ho Chi Minh City two thousand new enterprises sprang up in three months, producing metal goods, electrical fixtures, kitchenware, soap and cigarettes" (Thayer 1982, p. 42, citing Marr).

Further, the ethnic Chinese left in the city were involved in much of this new activity (Stern 1985). The thaw had immediate knock-on effects on the ownership of industry in the small industry and handicrafts sector. By May 1981, the city had 192 registered co-operatives and 2173 production teams employing nearly 95 000 workers in this sector. However, it also had 643 privately owned shops and 16 468 individually owned shops employing a further 60 000 workers. At the same time, the thaw meant that a steady growth in output was achieved in this sector, from 672 million dong in 1978 to 932 million dong in 1981 (*Vietnam Courier* 1982b).

By the end of 1982, however, it started to become apparent that things were getting out of hand in the city. In particular, the operations of a whole series of trading companies which had been set up came under suspicion:

> there were seventeen separate companies, one for each (precinct or) district, and also five city-wide companies; an export–import company called Cholemex, which was backed by the Chinese, had a capitalization of a billion dong, and a similar Vietnamese company had half that much. Starting from zero at the end of the war, an export–import trade of three hundred million dollars a year had been built up (Shaplen 1985a, p. 121).

These companies were bidding against each other, so adding to inflation in Ho Chi Minh City, and also pushing levels of corruption to new heights. Two of them were even run by ethnic Chinese (Stern 1985).

In late 1982 a special meeting of the Political Bureau was unusually held in Ho Chi Minh City and was very critical. As a result in early 1983 two government investigation teams, led by high-ranking officials, descended on the city and all trading was suspended while they conducted their investigations (*Far Eastern Economic Review* 1984). The results of the investigations led to the establishment of a single import–export concern called the General Export and Import Company, which co-ordinated procurement in the city and in the Southern provinces as a whole. However, the extent of the thaw is shown by the fact that the 17 district companies, and Cholemex, were allowed to resume supplying export commodities. Further, when Le Duan attended a party meeting of the municipal government of Ho Chi Minh City in late 1983, he "took much of the edge off the earlier criticism by praising city officials for their aggressive leadership and calling for Ho Chi Minh City to become an 'export city'" (Shaplen 1985a, p. 121). The market was most definitely resurgent.

The moral–internal security imperative has proved very problematic, especially against the background of increased market activity. In 1975, the immediate problems were solved easily enough. The city's estimated 130 000 prostitutes and 150 000 drug addicts were packed off for re-education and rehabilitation (McCoy 1983, p. 34), along with many members of the former régime. The city's administration was also revamped within a very short time. A ward block and cell system was instituted, and the socialization of citizens went ahead through a reformed educational system and a whole series of overlapping organizations, from labour unions to militias to women's groups,[13] under the umbrella of the National Fatherland Front. In Ho Chi Minh City the Front is currently active in all the 17 districts and precincts and reaches down through the various administrative levels to the thousands of block committees.

However, progress has not proved as quick as was once expected. "Cultural resistance" of a passive kind is still widespread:

By 1978 the (Vietnam Communist Party) was forming 'cultural army units' in each party chapter to launch an all-out attack on the remnants of 'neocolonialist culture'. This program could not have been successful . . ., for in May 1981 the Executive Committee of the Ho Chi Minh City Party Committee issued a directive to carry out a 'decisive struggle' . . . In implementing the directive, a three-day campaign launched in eleven precincts resulted in seizure of 'more than 2,500 phonograph records and cassettes, dozens of movie reels and over 4 tons of reactionary books . . .' In addition, 'owners of hundreds of coffee shops, and undercover music halls – the major threat to our society in the field of culture, literature and arts' – were 'appropriately punished'.

    . . . Also in May 1981, the party convened a meeting of all party officials in charge of culture, literature, and the arts in all the provinces of South Vietnam . . . All the delegates concluded that 'numerous negative phenomena' were appearing in the region's culture. As examples of such phenomena a reporter for Tien Phong magazine cited the latest songs by Pham Duy, Hung Cuong and other composers who had fled to the United States after the United States takeover. The songs were available in Ho Chi Minh City's numerous coffee houses. There, during the late evening, tables and chairs were stacked against the walls, rock music was played and people danced. Tran Quang Khai Street, in the city's first precinct, had 21 such coffee houses/dance halls. A raid on them in April had turned up, 'hundreds of tapes of decadent music' (Nguyen Van Canh 1983, pp. 148–9).

Periodic outbreaks of zealotry like these have continued (with little success). More serious have been two further developments. First, the growth of the free market has led to "negative phenomena", even amongst party members. This has caused much concern:

A (Vietnamese Communist Party) Politburo meeting was held in Hanoi in mid–August (1983) to receive and consider a report on the state of Party affairs in Ho Chi Minh City. The accounting was ordered by the Politburo, it appears, following appearance in the press and elsewhere of charges that the local *apparat* was guilty of various sins including corruption, inefficiency, nepotism and generally ignoring the directives of the Central Committee. The Politburo 'pointed out' shortcomings and weaknesses in Ho Chi Minh City Party performance in a statement that amounts to a highly unusual public dressing down . . . (*Indochina Chronology* 1983, 2(3), p. 8).

Secondly, there are indications of more serious resistance to the régime. In May 1983, two leaders of the Front for the National Liberation of Vietnam, an anti-government organization composed of ex-soldiers of the Republic of Vietnam, were executed in the city. Several Roman Catholics (including Jesuit priests) were amongst 13 anti-government plotters brought to trial in the city in April 1983. One man received a life sentence, six received sentences of between 3 and 15 years, two were put on probation and four were acquitted (Shaplen 1985b). In December 1984 a four-day show trial ended with the conviction of all the 21 defendants. Five were sentenced to death (although two later had their sentences commuted to life imprisonment), three were given life imprisonment and the remainder between 8 and 20 years in prison. The group included a French citizen, Catholics and members of the Cao-Dai and Hoa-Hao sects. Apparently about another 100 dissidents await trial (*Indochina Chronology* 1984, 3(4), p. 6). These kinds of events have served to increase suppression of any likely dissident group in the city – Catholics, Buddhists, the still sizeable ethnic Chinese community (numbering 480 000 or 14.5% of the city's population) (Stern 1985), the Cao-Dai, Hoa-Hao, and so on.

Certainly, however, Ho Chi Minh City has seen wide-ranging changes in the last ten years. These changes have not just been physical (the fabric of the city is certainly in need of attention): they have also been social. There are, every now and then, tantalizing glimpses of the impacts of the wide-ranging changes that have taken place on the social structure of the city. For example, the state administrative class is taking over the best areas of the city (Shaplen 1985b), and in the traditionally Chinese suburb of Cholon (with its many vacated and empty shop-houses) now that many of the wealthy and middle class Chinese have left, either under the orderly departure programme or as "boat people", the Chinese lower middle class are taking over (Shaplen 1985a). These are changes that would repay further research.

Notes

1 For a vivid account of which see Burchett (1956).
2 The city was run for a year by a joint military–civilian administrative committee, until 1957 by a Municipal Administrative Committee and from 1957 by a formally elected Municipal People's Council (Turley 1975b).
3 This was also a disadvantage, however. As has also been noted by Vogel (1969) in the instance of the communist take-over in Canton, the new revolutionary cadres did not always get on well with these civil servants.
4 The number of wards has since increased considerably.
5 It is interesting to note that, on average, the rate of Hanoi's population growth during the war years still slightly exceeded the national average. In-migration accounted for half of the annual average increase. In 1974, the growth rate for the city was 2.4% (Nguyen Duc Nhuan 1984a, p. 334).
6 Apart from the incessant bicycle traffic jams!
7 Some housing in Hanoi is still in private hands.
8 There was also a brief French occupation of the city in 1859.
9 Nguyen Duc Nhuan (1984a) gives a figure for average housing space in Ho Chi Minh City at $14 \, m^2$ per person, much higher than the comparable figure for Hanoi.
10 Vegetable acreage was also to be increased from the 1981 level of 2000 ha to 4000 ha. Animal husbandry was also actively encouraged. For example, in 1979 there were 160 000 pigs in the city but the target was 230 000 (Report of Australian Committee 1981).
11 Compare with the similar situations to be found at the time of the Communist take-over of Shanghai (see Barber 1979).
12 It is perhaps no surprise that in May 1978 many Chinese residents of Ho

Chi Minh City were killed in a clash with troops (see *Far Eastern Economic Review* 1979, p. 339). The rows and rows of closed Chinese shop-houses in the predominantly Chinese suburb of Cholon still testify to the extent of the attack on the ethnic Chinese at this time but the ethnic Chinese have been remarkably resilient. By 1981, for example, Dao Van Tap stated that Hoa merchants in Ho Chi Minh City again controlled 90% of the Southern rice trade (Stern 1985).

13 A number of books have documented the impacts of these changes on the everyday life of the citizens of Ho Chi Minh City (see Terzani 1976, Martin 1978; Hawthorne 1982, Nguyen Ngoc Ngan 1982).

10 Conclusions

There is no easy way to summarize the forces behind the Vietnamese experience of urbanization under socialism, given the constraints on what data are obtainable and our lack of any detailed understanding of much which has been outlined in the preceding chapters. However, even in the fragmented form in which the Vietnamese experience has been related, there are still lessons to be learnt about urbanization in socialist developing countries and especially how the Murray–Szelenyi (1984) model outlined in Chapter 3 approximates to this experience. Three important interconnected points can be made. These concern the state and the state's rôle in directing the economy, civil society and external relations.

STATE AND ECONOMY

Given the difficulties under which it works, the Vietnamese state is in many ways a remarkable set of apparatuses, responsible for numerous far-reaching transformations. However, it would be dangerous to make too much of the transformative power of the Vietnamese state. Vietnam is, after all, one of the poorest of the developing countries. The result is that the Vietnamese state is very much restrained in what it has been able to do and what it can do. The Vietnamese state operates under a number of constraints amongst which the most important is the *scarcity* of resources of all kinds, from capital to (at least in the South) loyal party members. There are many reasons for this scarcity of resources but two stand out. First, like many other developing countries, Vietnam has been and still is the prisoner of a race between population increase and finding the food to feed the increased population. Secondly, so many of the resources of the Vietnamese State are channelled into defence. This scarcity of resources makes the institution of a state based on centralized planning – and a subsequently high degree of co-ordination – problematic, to say the least. We do not intend to go

into all the problems there are in co-ordinating diverse state apparatuses in the face of shortages of paper, pens, etc. (see Forbes & Thrift
1986). Instead, the differences between an Eastern European socialist
state and a socialist developing country state like Vietnam can be
adequately described by means of a short vignette recounted by a
Vietnamese social psychologist:

> Vietnamese newspapers trying to ridicule unresponsive
> bureaucrats, depicted them as creatures riding telephones on
> their way to work. In other words, wrote Nguyen Duc Uy,
> such newspapers just assumed that Vietnamese bureaucrats
> must be like their brethren in other 'socialist countries' who
> were 'automatic machines' clinging 'tightly' to vast arrays of
> clearly documented, precise work regulations, and surrounded
> by piles of shrilly clamouring telephones. But in fact Vietnam
> had very few telephones (Woodside 1979, p. 401).

The result of this scarcity of resources is to exacerbate contradictions
that already exist in all socialist states and, in particular, the contradiction between plan and market: there is a constant see-sawing in
economic policy between the desire to plan and the need to produce.

Thus it would be wrong to depict the Vietnamese (or any other
socialist developing) state as a monolithic force able to have its way
on every issue, and this stricture applies to the case of state control of
the rate and pattern of urbanization as well as it does to any other
instance. For example, it is fairly easy to paint the re-organization of
space and population movements in Vietnam, with their direct
effects on the rate and pattern of urbanization, as stemming from an
elemental socialist power following a "Promethean strategy of constant mobilization of space and populations" that "redispersed
several millions of new city folk to work in the rural zones" (Nguyen
Duc Nhuan 1984a, p. 86). Discounting any element of exaggeration
here, it is important to remember that although such a strategy may
exist, the power of implementation is less certain. The impulses that
lie behind the re-organization of space and the allied population
movements may have originated within the state (as a response to
the exigencies of acting out the rôle of a developing country at war)
but the state has quite clearly not been able to channel these impulses
at it would have liked. The flow-back of those sent to the New
Economic Zones into Ho Chi Minh City is just one example here
among many.

   The major point is that by representing the power of the Vietnamese or any other socialist developing country state as equivalent to the power of socialist states in Eastern Europe (which itself is by no means unbounded) it becomes possible to misinterpret a particular rate and pattern of urbanization as being the result of conscious and decisive state action when, in many cases, it is not. It even becomes possible to read the wrong reason into why state actions took place. The Murray–Szelenyi model is in particular danger of doing just this when applied to, for example, the case of North Vietnam. Thus, the period of slow urban growth in North Vietnam from 1954 to 1965 was as much to do with the general lack of resources available to the North Vietnamese state to build factories and housing as it was with conscious action by a strong state to maximize industrialization and minimize urbanization. Hence the reasons that Murray and Szelenyi (1984) give as typical of a period of slow urban growth are mitigated by circumstances. In the case of the period of zero urban growth in North Vietnam from 1965 to 1973 the influence of warfare is the main causal element promoting this rate and pattern of urbanization. Certainly a "Maoist" rural in- dustrialization policy is in evidence but this was a policy forced on the Democratic Republic in response to war. In happier circum- stances the state would have much preferred a more concerted and centralized programme of industrialization. Certainly there is no evidence of any higher level of internal bureaucratic in-fighting than in any other socialist state. Here the reasons that Murray and Szelenyi (1984) give as typical of zero urban growth are subsidiary or even non-existent.

CIVIL SOCIETY

In all socialist developing countries the nature of civil society is still a crucial determinant of the state's ability to plan and control, and this stricture applies to the rate and pattern of urbanization as much as to any other focus of state intervention. For example, Vietnamese civil society has had important effects on urbanization under the socialist régime (although these effects are admittedly very difficult to sort out from other interdigitated influences). There are at least three points at which civil society and the rate and pattern of urbanization have interlocked. The first of these was in 1954 when the Roman Catholics made their exit from the North, a useful *de facto* de-urbanization. The second point of interlock was in the severe period of de-urbanization in the South of Vietnam, after 1978 in particular. If much of the middle class had not also been an identifiable ethnic group, the ethnic Chinese, originating from a country with which Vietnam has a long history of emnity, then it is doubtful that the de-urbanization would have been so severe. (Indeed the severity of the de-urbanization was such that it, in all probability, sparked off another chapter in this long history of mutual enmity, the Third Indochina War (see Woodside 1979, Evans & Rowley 1984).) Finally, a number of population movements in the South of Vietnam since 1975 have been concerned with inserting loyal populations into areas where there are troublesome or potentially troublesome ethnic minorities so providing defence against insurrection by dilution.

EXTERNAL RELATIONS

The importance of external relations in the history of so many socialist developing countries cannot be underestimated. In particular, the activity of warfare is crucial in building a sovereign national state and then maintaining it. Further, some of these countries (such as Vietnam) have what might be called "subimperialist aspirations" (Shaw 1984, p. 67) (as shown for example, by the adventures of the Socialist Republic of Vietnam in Cambodia), which exacerbate further any militarist tendencies. It should come as no surprise, then, to find that social processes in a number of socialist developing countries are, in Bienkowski's apposite term, "forced" by warfare. In turn, these war-directed social processes can have impacts on the rate and pattern of urbanization. In Vietnam this seems to be particularly the case.

The most obvious way in which these social processes in Vietnam have been forced by warfare has been direct – destruction (and consequent scarcity and shortages) and the reshuffling of populations on a grand scale. The effects of factors like these linger on long after war has ended in the shape of problems like housing shortages and high population densities. The history of Hanoi and the Northern cities illustrates this point particularly well. Warfare was directly reponsible for the period of zero urban growth from 1965 to 1973, but also had contributory effects in the period of slow urban growth before 1965. The history of Ho Chi Minh City and the Southern cities is no less the history of the effects of warfare on urbanization, not only in the period of "hyperurbanization" before 1975, but also in the period of de-urbanization thereafter.

However, the effects of warfare are not just to be found in destruction, scarcity and shortages or in the reshuffling of population – on however grand a scale. War has had more subtle effects on social relations as well. Thus the Second Indochina War forced "socialist principles" on to the state and the population as a matter of necessity, *not* as a matter of ideology. For example:

> the number of communal dining halls in the cities of the north increased in the 1960s, (in Haiphong from 434 in 1964 to 996 in 1970) not because of any real worship of a millenium of urban communes, as in China during the Great Leap Forward, but in order to save time and labour during the war (Woodside 1976, p. 265).

However, the Second Indochina War did not only have the effect of strengthening "socialist principles", it also sometimes weakened them. For example, as pointed out for Hanoi in Chapter 9, the large-scale industrial sector in the city took some time to set up and get running again after the war. Small-scale industry had to substitute, and this encouraged the growth of a free market which still operates in strength – "thus the war brought not only physical destruction but also backsliding on the road to socialism" (Turley 1975b, p. 391).

Another way in which social processes have been forced by warfare in Vietnam, with consequent effects on towns and cities, is perhaps the most difficult to trace, yet may be the most far-reaching. Vietnam is a society with a very high military participation ratio. The proportion of the Vietnamese population that is or has been mobilized for war is enormous. At present about 1 in every 57 of the population is a member of the army. This figure ignores the members of the population who are in the other armed forces, the reserves or the paramilitary forces like the People's Regional Force, the People's Self-defence Force and the Armed Youth Assault Force (which brings the figure down to perhaps 1 in 9).[1] Furthermore, it takes no note of those who have at some time in the past participated in the armed forces but are no longer associated with military activities. It is not too much of an exaggeration to say that Vietnamese society is used to war and that it is organized for war. (In many ways, its problem is how to demobilize.) Similarly, it follows that

Vietnam's high military participation ratio must have had effects on social organization and structure in the cities about which, as yet, we know all too little.

Finally, the possibility of warfare has exercised an almost continuous influence on the Vietnamese state; "internal and external policies form a seamless web of cause and effect" (Evans & Rowley 1984, p. 4). It has led directly to the massive defence budget for the armed forces which has, in turn, been crucial in directing resources away from other priorities, including industrialization and housing, with inevitable effects on the direction and pattern of urbanization. However, more than this, the element of defence has been a crucial factor in the state's direction of many population movements, most especially to the Chinese border but also to the Laotian and Kampuchean borders as well:

> Déplacer une dizaine de millions d'habitants des régions surpeuplées du nord et du Centre vers le delta du Mékong, les hauts plateaux du Centre et les Montagnes de Truong Son, non seulement par doubler nos surfaces cultivées mais également pour constituer des solides bases militaires en étroite liaison avec le système de défence de deux pays Frères du Laos et du Campuchea (*Tap Chi Cong San* 1979 cited in Nguyen Duc Nhuan 1984b, p. 321).

The influence of warfare on Vietnamese society and on Vietnamese urbanization has therefore been continuous and has had both direct and more subtle effects. These effects can be expected to continue to "force" Vietnamese social relations for many years to come.

SUMMARY

In summary, the Murray–Szelenyi model of urbanization in socialist countries is a useful model in so far as changes in the rate and pattern of urbanization can be traced to the interaction of state and economy. Certainly the state's imposition of its central planning and other rôles on the economy, with the corresponding changes in class relations, is an important force in dictating the rate and pattern of socialist urbanizations. However, it is important to remember that in socialist developing countries the state often lacks the power to direct the rate and pattern of urbanization as it would like, especially while civil society and external relations remain important determinants of urbanization. A full accounting of urbanization in socialist developing countires *must* include the elements of civil society and external relations, especially so long as these countries remain not only socialist but also nationalist (see Anderson 1983).

It is this final element of external relations between nation–states and its too common consequence – warfare – which has come to the fore as one of the most important determinants of Vietnamese urbanization under socialism. As this book has been written so the subject of warfare has written itself into the text. Vietnamese towns and cities have clearly paid the price of war and will continue to pay that price for some time to come. However, the theoretical and practical understanding of the combination of the building of the nation–state, warfare and the social effects of war remains in its early stages and has hampered our attempts at understanding the recent history of urbanization in Vietnam. It is therefore heartening to know that such an important topic as the nation–state and warfare is currently the subject of such intense interest in so many parts of social science.[2]

Notes

1 Taken from figures in *Far Eastern Economic Review* (1985).
2 See, for example, Calder (1969), Milward (1977), Shaw (1981, 1984), Hewitt (1982, 1983), Kidron and Smith (1983), Bond (1984), Douglas (1985), Giddens (1985), Thrift (1986).

Bibliography

Amin, S., G Arrighi, A. G. Frank, I. Wallerstein, 1982. *Dynamics of global crisis*. New York: Monthly Review Press.

Anderson, B. 1983. *Imagined communities: reflections on the origin and spread of nationalism*. London: Verso.

Andreski, S. 1968. *Military organisation and society*. Berkeley: University of California Press.

Andrusz, G. 1979. Some key issues in Soviet urban development. *International Journal of Urban and Regional Research*. **3**, 157–80.

Appleton, J. 1983. Socialist Vietnam: continuity and change. In *Rural development and the state*, Lea, D. A. M. and Chaudri, D. P. (eds). 254–82. London: Methuen.

Bahro, R. 1978. *The alternative in Eastern Europe*. London: New Left Books.

Banerjee, T. and S. Schenk 1984. Lower order cities and national urbanisation policies: China and India. *Environment and Planning A* **16**, 487–512.

Barber, N. 1979. *The fall of Shanghai*. New York: Coward, McCann & Geoghegan.

Barkin, D. 1978. Confronting the separation of town and country in Cuba. In *Marxism and the metropolis*, Sawers, L. and Tabb, W. (eds). New York: Oxford University Press.

Bettelheim, C. 1975. *The transition to socialist economy*. Hassocks: Harvester.

Bienkowski, W. 1981. *Theory and reality. The development of socialist systems*. London: Allison & Busby.

Bond, B. 1984. *War and society in Europe, 1870–1970*. London: Fontana.

Boudarel, G. 1970: L'évolution du statut de la femme dans la République Democratique du Vietnam. *Tiers Monde* **11** 42–3.

Boudarel, G. 1980. Influences and idiosyncracies in the line and practice of the Vietnamese Communist Party. In *Vietnamese communism in comparative perspective*, Turley, W. S. (ed.), 137–69. Boulder, Colorado: Westview Press.

Brittain, V. 1984. Africa's poor and honest have their day. *The Guardian*, August 7, 15.

Brus, W. 1972. *The market in a socialist economy*. London: Routledge and Kegan Paul.

Brus, W. 1975. *Socialist ownership and political systems*. London: Routledge and Kegan Paul.

Burchett, W. 1956. *North of the seventeenth parallel*. Delhi: People's Publishing House.

Byrnes, M. 1985a. China tops Hanoi's hate list. *Australian Financial Review*, January 14, 9–11.

Byrnes, M. 1985b. Why Hanoi is still in a state of war. *Australian Financial Review*, January 15, 9–10.

Byrnes, M. 1985c. The agonies of economic renaissance. *Australian Financial Review*, January 16, 9–12.

Byrnes, M. 1985d. Phnom Penh and the road back. *Australian Financial Review*, January 17, 9.

Calder, A. 1969. *The people's war. Britain 1939–1945*. London: Jonathan Cape.

Canberra Times 1983. Left-wing coup in Upper Volta. *Camberra Times*, August 6, 5.

Cao, A. D. 1978. Development planning in Vietnam: a problem of post-war transition. *Asia Quarterly* **4**, 263–76.

Castoriadis, C. 1973. *La société bureaucratique*. Paris: Éditions du Seuil.

Castoriadis, C. 1977. The social regime in Russia. *Telos* no. 38, 32–47.

Castoriadis, C. 1980. Socialism and autonomous society. *Telos* no. 45, 91–105.

Cell, C. 1980. The urban–rural contradiction in the Maoist era – the patterns of de-urbanization in China. *Comparative Urban Research* **21**, 48–62.

Central Committee 1977. *4th National Congress. Documents*. Hanoi: Foreign Languages Publishing House.

Central Committee 1982. Central Committee's political report. In *Summary of World Broadcasts*, Fe/6993/C/15, April 1.

Central Intelligence Agency 1981. *Handbook of economic statistics 1981*. Washington: National Foreign Assessment Centre.

Chanda, N. 1981a. A last minute rescue. *Far Eastern Economic Review*, February 27, 28–34.

Chanda, N. 1981b. Cracks in the edifice. *Far Eastern Economic Review*, December 4, 84–5.

Chanda, N. 1982a: Shake-up at the bottom. *Far Eastern Economic Review*, April 16, 15–17.

Chanda, N. 1982b: As Moscow's ardour cools, Hanoi looks elsewhere. *Far Eastern Economic Review*, April 18, 17–18.

Chanda, N. 1984: Toeing a liberal line. *Far Eastern Economic Review*, January 12, 32.

Chandler, D. P. and B. Kiernan (eds) 1983. *Revolution and its aftermath in Kampuchea*. Southeast Asian Monograph Series, no. 25. New Haven, Conn.: Yale University Press.

Chase-Dunn, C. K. (ed.) 1982. *Socialist states in the world-system*. Beverly Hills: Sage.

Clark, G. L and M. Dear 1984. *State apparatus. Structures and language of legitimacy*. London: Allen & Unwin.

Cliff, T. 1964. *State capitalism in Russia*. 1974 reprint. London: Pluto Press.

Cohen, J. L. 1982. *Class and civil society. The limits of Marxian critical theory*. Oxford: Martin Robertson.

Croll, E. 1979. *Socialist development experience: women in rural production and reproduction in the Soviet Union, China, Cuba and Tanzania.* University of Sussex Institute of Development Studies, Discussion Paper no. 143.

Dao Van Tap 1980. On the transformation and new distribution of population centres in the Socialist Republic of Vietnam. *International Journal of Urban and Regional Research* **4**, 503–15.

Decalo, S. 1981. People's Republic of Benin. In *Marxist governments: a world survey*, Szajkowski, B. (ed.), vol. 1, 87–115. London: Macmillan.

Demko, G. J. and R. J. Fuchs 1977. Commuting in the USSR and Eastern Europe. Causes, characteristics and consequences. *East European Quarterly* **9**, 463–75.

Donaldson, H. (ed.) 1981. *The Soviet Union in the Third World: successes and failures.* London: Croom Helm.

Douglas, J. N. H. 1985. Conflict between states. In *Progress in political geography*, Pacione, M. (ed.), 77–110. Beckenham: Croom Helm.

Downs, C. and F. Kusnetzoff 1982. The changing role of government in the Nicaraguan revolution. *International Journal of Urban and Regional Research* **6**, 533–48.

Duiker, W. J. 1980. *Vietnam since the fall of Saigon.* Ohio University Centre for International Studies, Southeast Asia Series, no. 56.

Duiker, W. J. 1981. *The communist road to power in Vietnam.* Boulder, Colorado: Westview Press.

Duiker, W. J. 1983. *Vietnam. Nation in revolution.* Boulder, Colorado: Westview Press.

Duiker, W. J. 1985. Vietnam in 1984. Between ideology and pragmatism. *Asian Survey* **25**, 97–105.

The Economist 1983a. Surinam: Cuba in miniature? January 8, 39.

The Economist 1983b. Destabilisation in Southern Africa. July 16, 15–28.

Eisen, A. 1985. *Women and revolution in Vietnam.* London: Zed Books.

Elias, N. 1982. *State formation and civilization.* Oxford: Blackwell.

Elliott, B. and D. McCrone 1982. *The City. Patterns of domination and conflict.* London: Macmillan.

Elliott, D. 1975. Political integration in North Vietnam: the cooperativisation period. In *Communism in Indochina: new perspectives*, Zasloff, J. and Brown, M. (eds), 165–94. Lexington, Mass.: D. C. Heath.

Elliott, D. 1976. *Revolutionary re-integration: a comparison of the foundation of post-liberation political systems in North Vietnam and China*, Unpublished PhD dissertation, Cornell University, Ithaca.

Elliott, D. 1980. *The Third Indochina War.* Boulder, Colorado: Westview Press.

Elliott, D. 1981. Socialist Republic of Vietnam. In *Marxist governments: a world survey*, Szajkowski, B. (ed.), vol. 3, 713–54. London: Macmillan.

Ellman, M. 1979. *Socialist planning.* Cambridge: Cambridge University Press.

Evans, G. and M. Rowley 1984. *Red brotherhood at war. Indochina since the fall of Saigon.* London: Verso.

Fall, B. B. 1967. *The two Vietnams: a political and military analysis*. London: Pall Mall Press.

Fallenbuchl, Z. M. 1977. Internal migration and economic development under socialism: the case of Poland. In *Internal migration: a comparative perspective*, Brown, A. A. and E. Neuberger, (eds), 305–27. New York: Academic Press.

Far Eastern Economic Review 1978. *Asia 1978 yearbook*. Hong Hong: Far Eastern Economic Review.

Far Eastern Economic Review 1979. *Asia 1979 yearbook*. Hong Kong: Far Eastern Economic Review.

Far Eastern Economic Review 1980. *Asia 1980 yearbook*. Hong Kong: Far Eastern Economic Review.

Far Eastern Economic Review 1981. *Asia 1981 yearbook*. Hong Kong: Far Eastern Economic Review.

Far Eastern Economic Review 1983a. *Asia 1983 yearbook*. Hong Kong: Far Eastern Economic Review.

Far Eastern Economic Review 1983b. Taming a wildcat. April 28, 54–5.

Far Eastern Economic Review 1984. *Asia 1984 yearbook*. Hong Kong: Far Eastern Ecomomic Review.

Far Eastern Economic Review 1985. *Asia 1985 yearbook*. Hong Kong: Far Eastern Economic Review.

Farina, M. B. 1980. Urbanisation, deurbanisation and class struggle in China 1949–79. *International Journal of Urban and Regional Research* **4**, 485–502.

Fenichel, A. and A. Khan 1981. The Burmese way to 'socialism'. In *Socialist models of development*, Jameson, K. P. and Wilber, C. K. (eds), 813–24. Oxford: Pergamon.

Feuchtwanger, E. J. and P. Nailor (eds) 1981. *The Soviet Union and the Third World*. London: Macmillan.

Fforde, A. J. 1982. *Problems of agricultural development in North Vietnam*. Unpublished PhD dissertation, Faculty of Economics, Cambridge University, Cambridge.

Fforde, A. J. 1983. *The historical background to agricultural collectivisation in North Vietnam*. Birkbeck College Department of Economics, Discussion Paper.

Firebrace, J. 1984. *Never kneel down. Drought, development and liberation in Eritrea*. Nottingham: Spokesman.

Forbes, D. K. & Thrift, N. J. 1982. *Decentralisation in Vietnam: a preliminary survey*. Australian National University Department of Human Geography, Seminar paper.

Forbes, D. K. and N. J. Thrift 1984. Town and city in Vietnam. *Vietnam Today* **28**, 3–7.

Forbes, D. K. and N. J. Thrift (eds) 1986a. *Urbanisation and territorial organisation in socialist developing countries*. Oxford: Blackwell.

Forbes, D. K. and N. J. Thrift 1986b. Territorial organisation, regional development and the city in Vietnam. In *Urbanisation and territorial organisation in socialist developing countries*, Forbes, D. K. and Thrift, N. J. (eds). Oxford: Blackwell.

Foucault, M. (1972). *The archaeology of knowledge*. Andover: Tavistock.

Foucault, M. 1977. *Discipline and punish*. London: Allen Lane.

Foucher, M. 1979: Enqûete au Nicaragua. *Hérodote* no. 16, 5–35.

Foucher, M. 1982. Le Bassin Mediterranéen d'Amerique: approches géo-politiques. *Hérodote* no. 27, 16–40.

Foucher, M. 1985. Problèmes strategiques et politiques de la Frontière Nord du Nicaragua. *Cahiers des Ameriques Latines* **1**, 69–89.

Frankel, B. 1983. *Beyond the state? Dominant theories and socialist strategies*. London: Macmillan.

Frankel, B. 1985. The historical obsolescence of market socialism. *Radical Philosophy* no. 39, 28–33.

Fraser, S. E. 1979. Notes on population and family planning in Vietnam. *Journal of Family Welfare* **25**, 69–82.

Fraser, S. E. 1981. Vietnam's 1980 census: current position and future outlook. *Contemporary Southeast Asia* **3**, 219–34.

Fraser, S. E. 1983. Vietnam: population statistics. *Vietnam Today* **24**, 8–10.

Fraser, S. E. 1985. Vietnam's population: current notes. *Contemporary Southeast Asia* **6**, 70–88.

French, R. A. and F. E. I. Hamilton (eds) 1979. *The socialist city*. Chichester: Wiley.

Gellner, E. 1983. *Nations and nationalism*. Oxford: Blackwell.

Giddens, A. 1981. *A contemporary critique of historical materialism*. London: Macmillan.

Giddens, A. 1985. *The nation state and violence*. Cambridge: Polity.

Goodman, A. E. and L. M. Franks 1975. The dynamics of migration to Saigon, 1964–1972. *Pacific Affairs* **48**, 199–214.

Gordon, A. 1981. North Vietnam's collectivisation campaigns: class struggle, production and the 'middle peasant'. *Journal of Contemporary Asia* **11**, 19–43.

Gottheil, F. 1981. Iraqi and Syrian socialism: an economic appraisal. In *Socialist models of development*, Wilber, C. K. and K. P. Jameson (eds) 825–37. Oxford: Pergamon.

Gouldner, A. 1979: *The future of intellectuals and the rise of the new class*. London: Macmillan.

Gourou, P. 1940. *L'utilization du sol en Indochine Francaise*. Paris: Centre d'Études de Politique Étrangère.

Gourou, P. 1965. *Les paysans du Delta Tonkinois*, new edn Paris: Mouton.

The Guardian 1983. Mozambique forces 'unproductive' into rural work. July 19, 3.

The Guardian 1984. Mozambique deals with unemployed. March 20, 6.

Gugler, J. 1978. A minimum of urbanism and a maximum of ruralism. *International Journal of Urban and Regional Research* **4**, 516–35.

Hastings, P. 1982. A tale of two cities. *Far Eastern Economic Review*, August 27, 30–3.

Hawthorne, L. (ed.) 1982. *Refugee. The Vietnamese experience*. Melbourne: Oxford University Press.

Hewitt, F. K. 1982. *Air war and the destruction of urban places*. Wilfred Laurier University Department of Geography, Research Paper no. 82/4.

Hewitt, F. K. 1983. Place annihilation: area bombing and the fate of urban places. *Annals of the Association of American Geographers* **73**, 257–94.
Hodgkin, T. 1981. *Vietnam. The revolutionary path*. London: Macmillan.
Holton, R. 1984. Cities and the transition to capitalism and socialism. *International Journal of Urban and Regional Research* **8**, 13–37.
Honey, P. J. 1979. A new light on Vietnam. Hoang Van Hoan's revelations. *China News Analysis*, October 26, 4–11.
Houtart, F. and G. Lemercinier 1984. *Hai Van. Life in a Vietnamese commune*. London: Zed Books.
Hue-Tam Ho Tai 1983. *Millenarianism and peasant politics in Vietnam*. Cambridge; Mass.: Harvard University Press.
Huynh Kim Khanh 1982. *Vietnamese communism 1925–1945*. Ithaca, New York: Cornell University Press.

Indochina Chronology (various issues). University of California, Berkeley.

Jameson, K. 1980. An intermediate regime in historical context: the case of Guyana. *Development and Change* **11**, 77–95.
Jones, G. W. 1982. Population trends and policies in Vietnam. *Population Development Review* **8**, 783–810.
Jones, G. W. and S. E. Fraser 1982. Population resettlement policies in Vietnam. In *Population resettlement programs in Southeast Asia*, Jones, G. W. and Richter, H. V. (eds), Development Studies Centre Monograph no. 30, 113–33. Canberra: Australian National University.

Kalecki, M. 1972. *Selected essays on the economic growth of the socialist and the mixed economy*. Cambridge: Cambridge University Press.
Karnow, S. 1983. *Vietnam. A history*. New York: Viking Press.
Kautsky, K. 1946. *Social democracy versus communism*. New York: Rand School Press.
Kidron, M. and D. Smith 1983. *The war atlas*. London: Heinemann.
Kiernan, B. 1985. *How Pol Pot came to power*. London: Verso.
Kiernan, B. and B. Chantou (eds) 1982. *Peasants and politics in Kampuchea 1942–1981*. London: Zed Press.
Konrad, G. and I. Szelenyi 1977. *The intellectuals on the road to class power*. Brighton: Harvester.
Kornai, J. 1980. *Economics of shortage*. Amsterdam: North Holland.

Lang, M. H. and B. Kolb 1980. Locational components of urban and regional public policy in postwar Vietnam: the case of Ho Chi Minh City (Saigon) *Geographical Journal* **4**(1), 13–18.
Le Hong Tam 1980. Development policy: providing the basics. *Southeast Asia Chronicles* **76**, 22–9.
Le Mong Nguyen 1971. Étude du rôle social, économique et politique des agglomerations au Vietnam. In *Les Agglomerations Urbaines dans les Pays du Tier Monde*, Brussels: International Institute of Differing Civilisations.
Lefort, C. 1974. What is bureaucracy? *Telos* no. 22, 31–65.

Leifer, M. 1981. The Soviet Union in South-East Asia. In *The Soviet Union and the Third World*, Feuchtwanger, E. J. and Nailor, P. (eds), 164–182. London: Macmillan.

Lenin, V. I. 1964. *Selected works*, vol. 23. Moscow: Progress.

Lewis, J. 1982. *Sand reform or socialist agriculture. Rural development in PDR Yemen 1967–82*. Australian National University Department of Human Geography, Seminar Paper.

Limqueco, P. and B. MacFarlane 1980. Problems of economic planning for underdeveloped socialist countries. In *Planning Industrial Development*, Walker, D. F. (ed.), 47–70. Chichester: Wiley.

Löwy, M. 1981. *The politics of combined and uneven development. The theory of permanent revolution*. London: New Left Books.

MacKenzie, D. 1983: Militarism and socialist theory. *Capital and Class* no. **19**, 33–73.

Mandel, E. 1974. Ten theses on the social and economic laws governing the society transitional between capitalism and socialism. *Critique* **3**, 21–8.

Marr, D. 1971. *Vietnamese anticolonialism 1895–1925*. Berkeley: University of California Press.

Marr, D. 1981. *Vietnamese tradition on trial 1920–1940*. Berkeley: University of California Press.

Marr, D. 1982. *Both war and peace: life in Vietnam since 1975*. Griffith University, School of Modern Asian Studies, Centre for the Study of Australian Asian Relations, Research Paper no. 20.

Martin, E. S. 1978. *Reaching the other side. The journal of an American who stayed to witness Vietnam's post-war transition*. New York: Crown.

Marwick, A. 1968. *Britain in the century of total war*. London: Bodley Head.

McCoy, A. 1983. A tale of three cities. Hanoi, Saigon and Phnom Penh. *Geo: Australasia's Geographical Magazine* **5**(2), 28–40.

Miller, E. W. 1947. Industrial resources of Indochina. *Far Eastern Quarterly* **6**, 395–408.

Milward, A. S. 1977. *War, economy and society 1939–1945*. London: Allen Lane.

Mingione, E. 1981. *Social conflict and the city*. Oxford: Blackwell.

Moise, E. E. 1976. Land reform and land reform errors in North Vietnam. *Pacific Affairs* **49**, 70–92.

Molyneux, M. 1981. Women in socialist societies. Problems of theory and practice. In *Of Marriage and the market. Women's subordination in international perspective*, Young, K., Wolkowitz, C. and McCullagh, R. (eds), 167–202: London: CSE Books.

Monnier, A. 1981. Données recentes sur la population du Vietnam. *Population* **36**, 610–19.

Morrow, M. 1982. Ready for a rebound. *Far Eastern Economic Review*. January 29, 48–9.

Murray, M. 1980. *The development of capitalism in colonial Indochina (1780–1940)*. Berkeley: University of California Press.

Murray, M. and P. Picha 1982. Why make a socialist revolution? The case of

Vietnam. In *Socialist states in the world-system*, Chase-Dunn, C. D. (ed.), 253–67. Beverly Hills: Sage.

Murray, P. and I. Szelenyi 1982. *The city in the transition to socialism*. Paper prepared for the Xth World Congress of Sociology, Mexico City. Unpublished.

Murray, P. and I. Szelenyi 1984. The city in the transition to socialism. *International Journal of Urban and Regional Research* **8**, 330–50.

Musil, J. 1980. *Urbanisation in socialist countries*. White Plains, New York: M. E. Sharpe.

Musil, J. and Z. Rysavy. 1983. Urban and regional processes under socialism and capitalism: a case study from Czechoslovakia. *International Journal of Urban and Regional Research* **7**, 495–527.

Nayver, D. (ed.) 1977. *Economic relations between socialist countries and the Third World*. London: Macmillan.

Ng Shui Meng 1974. *The population of Indochina*. Singapore: Institute of Southeast Asian Studies.

Nguyen Duc Nhuan 1977. *Désurbanisation et développement régional au Vietnam (1954–1977)*. Paris: Centre de Sociologie Urbaine.

Nguyen Duc Nhuan 1978. Désurbanisation et développement régional au Vietnam (1955–77). *International Journal of Urban and Regional Research* **2**, 330–50.

Nguyen Duc Nhuan 1982a. *Héritage au residu mandarinal dans la politique communiste d'amenagement urbain et régional au Viet Nam*. Paper presented to the Xth World Congress of Sociology, Mexico City. Unpublished.

Nguyen Duc Nhuan 1982b. Les contradictions de l'organisation scientifique de l'espace et du travail agricoles au Nord-Vietnam 1954–1981. *L'Espace Géographique* **11**, 81–94.

Nguyen Duc Nhuan 1984a. Do the urban and regional policies of socialist Vietnam reflect the patterns of the ancient Mandarin bureaucracy? *International Journal of Urban and Regional Research* **8**, 78–89.

Nguyen Duc Nhuan 1984b. Contraintes démographiques et politiques de développement au Vietnam 1975–1980. *Population* **36**, 313–38.

Nguyen Huu Dong 1982. Collective and family agriculture in socialist economies. *Bulletin of the Institute of Development Studies* **13**(4), 23–8.

Nguyen Khac Vien (ed.) 1971. *General education in the D.R.V.N.* Vietnamese Studies, no. 30. Hanoi: Foreign Languages Publishing House.

Nguyen Khac Vien 1982a Ho Chi Minh City – 1982: the releasing process. *Vietnam Courier* **18**(4), 20–3.

Nguyen Khac Vien 1982b. The Vietnamese economy. *Journal of Contemporary Asia* **12**, 376–81.

Nguyen Nga Nio 1982. New measures for improving economic management. *Vietnam Courier* **18**(2), 8–10.

Nguyen Ngoc Ngan 1982. *The will of heaven. A story of one Vietnamese and the end of his world*. New York: Dutton.

Nguyen Thy 1974. Urbanisation processes in North Vietnam. *Soviet Geography* **15**, 352–7.

Nguyen Tien Hung 1977. *Economic development of socialist Vietnam, 1955–80.* New York: Praeger.

Nguyen Van Canh 1983. *Vietnam under communism, 1975–1982.* Stanford, California: Hoover Press.

Nove, A. 1979. *Political economy and Soviet socialism.* London: Allen & Unwin.

Nove, A. 1983. *The economics of feasible socialism.* London: Allen & Unwin.

Nove, A. 1985a Beyond the market? Comments on Boris Frankel. *Radical Philosophy* no. 39, 24–7.

Nove, A. 1985b. Response to Boris Frankel's reply. *Radical Philosophy*, no. 39, 34–5.

Nove, A. and D. M. Nuti (eds) 1972. *Socialist economics.* London: Penguin.

Nuti, D. M. 1979. The contradictions of socialist economies: a Marxist interpretation. In *The socialist register, 1979,* Miliband, R. and Saville, J. (eds), 228–73. London: Merlin.

Nyland, C. 1981: Vietnam, the plan/market contradiction and the transition to socialism. *Journal of Contemporary Asia* 11, 426–48.

O'Connor, A. 1985. *The African city.* London: Hutchinson.

Ofer, G. 1977. Economising on urbanisation in socialist countries: historical necessity or socialist strategy? In *Internal migration: a comparative perspective,* Brown, A. A. and Neuberger, E. (eds.) 277–303. New York: Academic Press.

Ollman, B. 1977. Marx's vision of communism: a reconstruction. *Critique* 8, 4–42.

Ottaway, D. and M. Ottaway (eds) 1981. *Afrocommunism.* New York: Holmes & Meier.

Pallot, J. and D. J. B. Shaw 1981. *Planning in the Soviet Union.* London: Croom Helm.

Paxton, J. (ed.) 1981. *The statesman's yearbook 1981–82.* London: Macmillan.

Pham Van Dong 1982. Premier's economic report to Fifth Vietnamese Party Congress. In *Summary of World Broadcasts,* FE/6991/C.1, March 30. London: British Broadcasting Corporation.

Pike, D. 1982. Vietnam in 1981: biting the bullet. *Asian Survey* 22, 69–77.

Popkin, S. L. 1979. *The Rational Peasant.* Berkeley: University of California Press.

Pressat, R. 1974. Quelques données sur la population du Vietnam du Sud. *Population* 29, 633–41.

Quinn-Judge, P. 1982. Combat fatigue sets in. *Far Eastern Economic Review,* May 28, 26–7.

Quinn-Judge, P. 1983a. Tightening the rein. *Far Eastern Economic Review,* July 14, 70–1.

Quinn-Judge, P. 1983b. Ideological backtracking. *Far Eastern Economic Review,* July 21, 23.

Quinn-Judge, P. 1985. No more free lunch. *Far Eastern Economic Review,* July 25, 36–7.

Racine, A. 1982. The People's Republic of Benin. In *The new communist Third World*, Wiles, P. J. (ed.), 205–29. London: Croom Helm.

Renaud, B. 1981. *National urbanization policy in developing countries*. New York: World Bank and Oxford University Press.

Report of Australian Committee 1981. Report on discussions held with the Social Sciences Committee of Vietnam and others during a visit to Vietnam and Kampuchea by an academic legation of the Australian Committee for Scientific Co-operation with Vietnam, August 19 to September 9, 1981.

Rev, I. 1984. Local autonomy or centralism – when was the original sin committed?, *International Journal of Urban and Regional Research* 8, 38–63.

Robequain, C. 1944. *The economic development of French Indo-China*. London: Oxford University Press.

Rogers, A. and J. G. Williamson (eds) 1982. Urbanization and development in the Third World. *Economic Development and Cultural Change* 30(1).

Rogge, J. R. 1985. The Indo-Chinese diaspora: where have all the refugees gone? *Canadian Geographer* 29, 65–72.

Schnytzer, A. 1982. The Socialist Republic of Vietnam. In *The New Communist Third World*, Wiles, P. (ed.), 342–55. London: Croom Helm.

Selucky, R. 1979. *Marxism, socialism and freedom. Towards a general theory of democratic systems*. London: Macmillan.

Shabad, T. 1958. Economic developments in North Vietnam. *Pacific Affairs* 31(1), 36–53.

Shaplen, R. 1985a. Return to Vietnam 1, *The New Yorker*, April 22, 104–25.

Shaplen, R. 1985b. Return to Vietnam 2, *The New Yorker*, April 29, 92–115.

Shaw, M. 1981. *Socialism and militarism*. Nottingham: Spokesman.

Shaw, M. (ed.) 1984. *War, state and society*. London: Macmillan.

Shawcross, W. 1981. The people of the two Vietnams. *New Society*, October 8, 56–9.

Shawcross, W. 1984. *The quality of mercy: Cambodia, holocaust and modern conscience*, London: Deutsch.

Sisaye, S. 1983. Urban industrial development in Ethiopia. *International Journal of Urban and Regional Research* 7, 528–58.

Skocpol, T. 1979. *States and social revolutions. A comparative analysis of France, Russia and China*. Cambridge: Cambridge University Press.

Slater, D. 1982. State and territory in Cuba. *International Journal of Urban and Regional Research* 6, 1–34.

Slater, D. 1985. Socialism, democracy and the territorial imperative – notes for a comparison of the Cuban and Nicaraguan experience. Paper presented to the International Sociological Association Conference on the Urban and Regional Impact on the New International Division of Labour, Hong Kong. Unpublished.

Smith, R. B. 1983. *An international history of the Vietnam war*. Vol. 1: *Revolution versus containment 1955–61*. London: Macmillan.

Snepp, F. 1977. *Decent interval*. New York: Random House.

Socialist Republic of Vietnam 1980. *The Socialist Republic of Vietnam*. Hanoi: Foreign Languages Publishing House.

Socialist Republic of Vietnam 1981. *Statistical data on the Socialist Republic of Vietnam, 1980.* Hanoi: Foreign Languages Publishing House.

Stern, C. M. 1985. The overseas Chinese in the Socialist Republic of Vietnam, 1979–82. *Asian Survey* **25**, 521–36.

Subcommittee on Immigrant and Refugee Policy 1982. *Refugee problems in Southeast Asia, 1981.* Washington: US Government.

Summary of World Broadcasts 1981. London: British Broadcasting Corporation.

Susman, P. 1974. Cuban development: from dualism to integration. *Antipode* **6**(3), 10–29.

Szajkowski, B. (ed.) 1981. *Marxist governments. A world survey.* London: Macmillan.

Szelenyi, I. 1978. Social inequalities under state socialist redistributive economies. *International Journal of Urban and Regional Research* **2**, 63–87.

Szelenyi, I. 1981a. The relative autonomy of the state or state mode of production? In *Urbanization and urban planning in capitalist society*, Dear, M. and Scott, A. J. (eds), 565–91. London: Methuen.

Szelenyi, I. 1981b. Urban development and regional management in Eastern Europe. *Theory and Society* **10**, 169–206.

Szelenyi, I. 1983. *Urban social inequalities under state socialism.* Oxford: Pergamon.

Szelenyi, I. 1984. Cities and the problem of the transition: introduction and rejoinder. *International Journal of Urban and Regional Research* **8**, 1–12.

Terzani, T. 1976. *Giai Phong! The fall and liberation of Saigon.* New York: St Martin's Press.

Thayer, C. A. 1982. *Building socialism. South Vietnam since the fall of Saigon.* Griffith University School of Modern Asian Studies, Centre for the Study of Australian Asian Relations, Research Paper no. 20.

Theriot, L. H. and J. Matheson 1979. Soviet economic relations with the non-European CMEA: Cuba, Vietnam and Mongolia. In *The Soviet economy in a time of change.* Washington: Central Intelligence Agency.

Thrift, N. J. 1983. On the determination of social action in space and time. *Environment and Planning D. Society and Space* **1**, 23–58.

Thrift, N. J. 1986. Little games and big stories. Accounting for the practice of personality and politics in the 1945 General Election. In *Politics, geography and social stratification*, Hoggart, K. and Kofman, E. (eds.) London: Croom Helm.

Thrift, N. J. and D. K. Forbes 1983. A landscape with figures: political geography with human conflict. *Political Geography Quarterly* **2**(3), 247–64.

Thrift, N. J. and D. K. Forbes 1985. Cities, socialism and war. Hanoi, Saigon and the Vietnamese experience of urbanisation. *Environment and Planning D. Society and Space* **3**, 279–308.

Ton That Thien 1983. Vietnam's new economic policy. *Pacific Affairs* **56**, 691–711.

Trullinger, J. B. Jr 1980. *Village at war. An account of revolution in Vietnam.* New York: Longman.

Turley, W. S. 1975a. The political role and development of the People's Army of Vietnam. In *Communism in Indochina: New Perspectives*, Zasloff, J. J. and Brown, M. (eds), 135–64. Lexington, Mass: D. C. Heath.

Turley, W. S. 1975b. Urbanization in war: Hanoi, 1947–1973. *Pacific Affairs* **48**, 370–96.

Turley, W. S. 1977a. Urban transformation in South Vietnam. *Pacific Affairs* **49**, 607–24.

Turley, W. S. 1977b. Vietnam since reunification. *Problems of Communism* **26**(2), 36–54.

Turley, W. S. (ed.) 1980a. *Vietnamese communism in comparative perspective*. Boulder, Colorado: Westview Press.

Turley, W. S. 1980b. Hanoi's domestic dilemmas. *Problems of Communism* **29**(4), 42–61.

United Nations 1980. *Patterns of urban/rural population growth*. New York: United Nations.

United Nations Development Programme 1981. *UNDP assistance requested by the government of Vietnam for the period 1982–1986*. UNDP document no. DP/GC/VIE/R.2. New York: United Nations.

United Nations Fund for Population Activities 1978. *Vietnam*. Report of Mission on Needs Assessment for Population Assistance, no. 2. New York: UNFPA.

United Nations Fund for Population Activities 1981. *Vietnam*. Report of Mission on Needs Assessment for Population Assistance, no. 3. New York: UNFPA.

Urry, J. 1981. *The anatomy of capitalist societies. The economy, civil society and the state*. London: Macmillan.

US Government 1967. *Area handbook of North Vietnam*. Washington: US Government.

United States Committee for Refugees, 1983. *World refugee survey 1983*. New York: USCR.

Vajda, A. 1981. *The state and socialism: Political essays*. London: Allison & Busby.

Vickery, M. 1984. *Cambodia 1975–1982*. Boston, Mass.: South End Press.

Vietnam Courier 1974a. Hanoi, one year after. *Vietnam Courier* **20**(3), 4–7.

Vietnam Courier 1974b. Transfer of population to new economic areas. *Vietnam Courier* **20**(7), 14–15.

Vietnam Courier 1980. The differences between the Vietnamese and the Chinese revolution. *Vietnam Courier* **16**(10), 8–12.

Vietnam Courier 1982a. Government report at 1981/1982 National Assembly. *Vietnam Courier* **18**(1), 3–5.

Vietnam Courier 1982b. Economic achievements in five years (1976–1980). *Vietnam Courier* **18**(2), 6–8.

Vietnam Courier 1982c. Housing – a real problem. *Vietnam Courier* **18**(4), 29.

Vietnam Courier 1982d. Socio-economic problems as seen by the Congress. *Vietnam Courier* **18**(5), 6–10.

Vietnam Courier 1982e. Special issue on Hanoi. *Vietnam Courier* **18**(10), 12–31.

Vietnam Courier 1984. Building up the district echelon: all-round development for 400 districts. *Vietnam Courier* **20**(10), 8–12.

Vietnam Courier 1985. Vietnam: some data. *Vietnam Courier* **21**(1), 25.

Vietnam Today 1984. IMF report on Vietnam's economy. *Vietnam Today* **28**, 7.

Vogel, E. F. 1969. *Canton under communism. Programs and politics in a provincial capital, 1949–1968.* Cambridge, Mass.: Harvard University Press.

Vu Tu Lap 1977. *Vietnam. Données géographiques.* Hanoi: Foreign Languages Publishing House.

Wallerstein, I. 1984. Cities in socialist theory and capitalist praxis. *International Journal of Urban and Regional Research* **8**, 64–72.

Werner, J. 1981. Women, socialism, and the economy of wartime North Vietnam, 1960–1975. *Studies in Comparative Communism* **14**(2–3), 165–90.

Westing, A. H. 1983. The environmental aftermath of warfare in Viet Nam. *Natural Resources Journal* **23**, 365–89.

Westing, A. H. 1984. *Herbicides in war. The long-term human and ecological consequences.* London: Taylor and Francis.

White, C. P. 1978. The peasants and the party in the Vietnamese Revolution. In *Peasants and politics. Grassroots reactions to changes in Asia.* Miller, D. B. (ed.) 19–49. Melbourne: Edward Arnold.

White, C. P. 1981. *Agrarian reform and national-liberation in the Vietnamese revolution, 1920–1957.* Ann Arbor: University Microfilms.

White, C. P. 1982a. *Debates in Vietnamese development policy*, University of Sussex, Institute of Development Studies, Discussion Paper no. 171.

White, C. P. 1982b. Socialist transformation of agriculture and gender relations: the Vietnamese case. *Bulletin of the Institute of Development Studies* **13**(4), 44–51.

White, C. P. 1983. Recent debates in Vietnamese development policy. In *Revolutionary socialist development in the Third World*, White, G., Murray, R. and White, C. (eds), 234–70. Brighton: Wheatsheaf.

White, C. P. 1984. Mass mobilisation and ideological transformation in the Vietnamese land reform campaign. *Journal of Contemporary Asia* **14**, 74–90.

White, C. P. and G. White (eds) 1982. Agriculture, the peasantry and socialist development. *Bulletin of the Institute of Development Studies*, **13**(4), 23–31.

White, G. 1983. Revolutionary socialist development: an overview. In *Revolutionary socialist development in the Third World*. White, G., Murray, R., and White, C. (eds), 1–34. Brighton: Wheatsheaf.

White, G. 1984. Developmental states and socialist industrialisation in the Third World. *Journal of Development Studies* **21**, 97–120.

White, G., R. Murray and C. White (eds) 1983. *Revolutionary socialist development in the Third World.* Brighton: Wheatsheaf.

Wiegersma, N. 1983. Regional differences in socialist transformation in Vietnam. *Economics Forum* **14**(1), 95–109.

Wilber, C. K., and K. P. Jameson (eds) 1982. *Socialist models of development*. Oxford: Pergamon.

Wiles, P. and A. Smith 1981. The commercial policies of the communist Third World. In *The Soviet Union and the Third World*, Feuchtwanger, E. and Nailor, P. (eds) 79–116. London: Macmillan.

Wiles, P. D. (ed.) 1982. *The new communist Third World*. London: Croom Helm.

Wolf, E. R. 1982. *Europe and the people without history*. Berkeley: University of California Press.

Woodside, A. 1971a. *Vietnam and the Chinese model: a comparative study of the Vietnamese and Chinese governments in the first half of the nineteenth century*. Cambridge: Mass.: Harvard University Press.

Woodside, A. 1971b. Decolonization and agricultural reform in Northern Vietnam. *Asian Survey* **10**, 705–23.

Woodside, A. 1976. *Community and revolution in modern Vietnam*. Boston: Houghton Mifflin.

Woodside, A. 1979. Nationalism and poverty in the breakdown of Sino-Vietnamese relations. *Pacific Affairs* **52**, 381–409.

World Bank 1982. *World development report 1982*. New York: Oxford University Press.

World Bank 1983. *World development report 1983*. New York: Oxford University Press.

Zaleski, E. 1980. *Stalinist planning for economic growth*. London: Macmillan.

Zasloff, J. J. and M. Brown (eds) 1975. *Communism in Indochina*. Lexington, Mass.: Lexington Books.

Zelinsky, W. 1950. The Indochinese peninsula – a demographic anomaly. *Far Eastern Quarterly*, **9**, 115–45.

Index